THE KIDS' BOOK

OF THE

AMERICAN QUARTER HORSE

Also by Steven D. Price

Teaching Riding at Summer Camp

Panorama of American Horses

Get a Horse!: Basics of Backyard Horsekeeping

Take Me Home: The Rise of Country-and-Western Music

The Second-Time Single Man's Survival Handbook
(with William J. Gordon)

Old as the Hills: The Story of Bluegrass Music

Horseback Vacation Guide

Schooling to Show: Basics of Hunter-Jumper Training
(with Antonio D'Ambrosio Jr.)

The Whole Horse Catalog
(with Barbara Burn, Gail Rentsch, Werner Rentsch, and David A. Spector)

Riding's a Joy
(with Joy Slater)

All the King's Horses: The Story of the Budweiser Clydesdales

Riding for a Fall

The Polo Primer
(with Charles Kauffman)

The Ultimate Fishing Guide

Caught Me a Big 'Un
(with Jimmy Houston)

The American Quarter Horse: An Introduction to Selection,
Care, and Enjoyment

The Quotable Horse Lover

THE KIDS' BOOK
OF THE
AMERICAN QUARTER HORSE

Steven D. Price

Illustrated by Rushe Hudson

THE LYONS PRESS
Guilford, Connecticut
An imprint of The Globe Pequot Press

AQHA MISSION

To record and preserve the pedigrees of the American Quarter Horse while maintaining the integrity of the breed;

To provide beneficial services for its members which enhance and encourage American Quarter Horse ownership and participation;

To generate growth of AQHA membership via the marketing, promotion, advertising, and publicity of the American Quarter Horse.

The Lyons Press is an imprint of The Globe Pequot Press.

Designed by SR Desktop Services, Ridge, NY
Photographs courtesy of the American Quarter Horse Association

Library of Congress Cataloging-in-Publication Data
Price, Steven D.
    The kids' book of the American quarter horse / Steven D. Price.
        p.   cm.
    Summary: Discusses the anatomy of American quarter horses, history of the breed, tips on riding, advice on selecting and caring for a quarter horse, and more.
    ISBN 1-55821-975-7 (pbk.)
    1. Quarter horse Juvenile literature.   [1. Quarter horse. 2. Horses.]   I. Title.
SF293.Q3P755   1999
636.1'33—dc21

                                                                99-34868
                                                                    CIP

Manufactured in the United States of America
First Edition/Second Printing

Contents

INTRODUCTION—
MEET TWO BITS

Hi, everybody! My name is Two Bits. Some of you may know me from *The Quarter Horse Journal* magazine. But if you don't know me, let me introduce myself: I'm an American Quarter Horse.

The American Quarter Horse is a breed of horse. A breed is a lot like a big family because all the animals that belong to the breed have the same great-great-great-grandparents. They also look alike, the way people in a human family often look alike.

There are lots of other breeds besides American Quarter Horses, and some horses are combinations of two or more breeds. But I think American Quarter Horses are very special. Not just because I'm one, but for the many reasons you'll find in this book.

We'll begin to learn about American Quarter Horses the way many young people do: by riding them and by watching them at horse shows and at racetracks.

Then we'll talk about ways you can get an American Quarter Horse of your own. If you keep one at home, you'll need to know how to care for him, so I'll give you some good ideas about taking care of a horse.

At every step along the way, I'll tell you about books, magazines, and videos where you can find out more information.

In this book you'll find many words having to do with horses and caring for horses that you're not familiar with. You can find out what these words mean at the back of this book in the part called the glossary. A glossary tells you the meanings of words you might not know. It also shows you how to say the words.

Okay? Everybody ready? Then let's saddle up and learn about . . .

The American Quarter Horse!

1

WHAT IS A HORSE?

Hi, it's me again, Two Bits. And I can hear you asking yourselves, "What kind of question is: 'What is a horse'? Everybody knows what a horse is."

In one sense, you're right. A horse is an animal that looks like a horse. A horse sounds like a horse and moves like a horse. A horse even smells like a horse.

Okay, let's ask the question another way. What are all the things that make a horse a horse? That's a little harder to answer, isn't it? There are so many things to think about.

The best way to start learning about horses is to look at one. You see, when it comes to learning about horses, your best teachers are horses themselves. Since I know a little something about the subject, I'll be your teacher today. You can call me Professor Two Bits.

We'll want to learn the parts of the horse. Some parts are things that everyone has heard of, like the mane and the tail.

But there are lots of other parts too. How many parts do you already know and how many are new to you?

Each part of the horse has a job to do. Let's go through the important parts. We'll start from the bottom up.

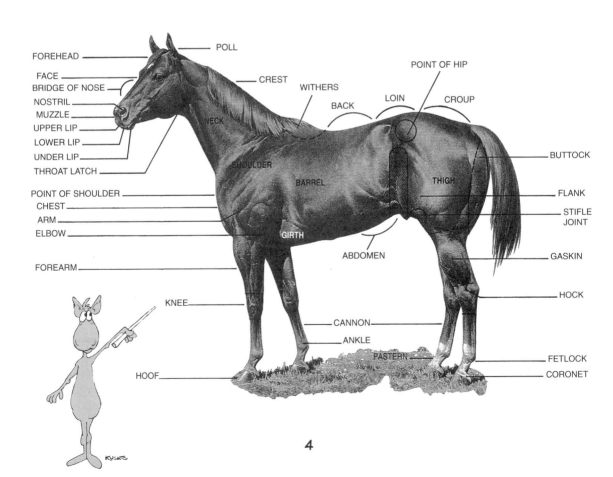

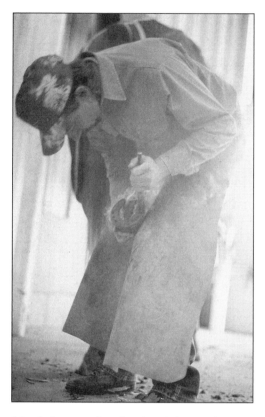

Metal shoes are first fitted and then nailed onto the horse's hooves. The person who does this job is called a farrier. (AQHA photo by Wyatt McSpadden)

Around each foot is a hard wall called the hoof. Two or more of them are called hooves. Like your fingernails, hooves grow a little bit every day. They need to be trimmed every month or so. And just like trimming a fingernail, trimming a hoof doesn't hurt.

Hooves are hard, but rocks and roads are harder. That's why horses wear shoes made of metal. A person called a farrier fits the shoe and then nails it onto the hoof. Don't worry, nailing a shoe on the hoof doesn't hurt a horse one bit.

Horses have frogs. No, not the green hopping kind that go "ribbit." The soft bottom of the horse's foot is called the frog. The hoof and the horseshoe keep the frog from being hurt by rocks and hard ground.

The hoof and the foot come together at a place called the coronet. Above the coronet is the fetlock. The fetlock bends the way your wrist does.

Each leg has two sets of long bones. The bones of the front legs are the forearm and the cannon. They come together at the knee. A horse's knee bends just the way your knee does.

The bones of the hind legs are called the gaskin and the cannon. We American Quarter Horses have short cannon bones. Short cannons help us make quick starts, turns, and stops.

The gaskin and cannon meet at a place called the hock. The hock works the way your elbow does. The gaskin connects with the body at the stifle. The stifle works the way your hip does.

The hard little lump on the inside of each leg is called the chestnut. If you look closely at lots of chestnuts, you will see that they look different on every horse. That's how they can be used to tell horses apart, just the way people's fingerprints can be used to tell people apart.

A horse's body is divided into three parts. The middle part of the horse's body is called the barrel. That's where the saddle goes. The part behind the barrel is the hindquarters. That's made up of the loin and the croup.

The top of the tail is called the dock. The dock has a muscle that lets the horse move his tail. Horses use their tail to push away flies. They also use it to let you know that something is bothering them.

The forehand is the part of the horse's body in front of where the saddle goes. The highest place of the body, where the neck meets the body, is called the withers. To tell how tall a horse is, you can measure from the withers down along his front leg to the ground. Horses are measured in units called hands. One hand equals four inches. Full-grown American Quarter Horses are about five feet tall at the withers, so five feet (which is sixty inches) measures fifteen hands.

The forelegs join the body at the shoulder. A horse that has a sloping shoulder will have a nice long stride. That will make him comfortable to ride.

The horse has a long neck that he can move easily. That lets him reach down to eat grass on the ground or reach up to get at leaves on trees way above his head. A horse can bend his neck so far, his head can reach all the way back almost to his tail. That lets him chase away bugs that his tail can't reach.

That clump of hair that hangs down the horse's forehead is called the forelock. Like the mane, it grows the way the hair on your head does. You'll learn about how we horses get our hair cut later in this book.

Did you know that horses have the largest eyes of any animal that lives on land? Well, we do. A horse's eyes are set back on either side of the head, not close together the way yours are. That spread-out position lets a horse see far behind him. However, with eyes that far apart, there's a spot in front of the horse's face and under his nose where he can't see anything. The only way he can see what's there is by lifting or turning his head.

Horses see differently in other ways too. They have trouble telling what's close-up and what's far away. That's why a horse turns his head when he gets close to an object, so he can tell how near or how far away he is from it.

Horses see things larger than they really are. Humans look nine or ten feet tall! Even small children look like grown-ups!

Unfortunately, a horse can't enjoy the colors on that pretty striped saddle blanket he's wearing. That's because all horses are color-blind. We can't tell colors apart. Everything is black, white, or a shade of gray.

A horse's eyes get used to changes in light more slowly than your eyes do. Whenever a horse moves from dark shadows to bright sunshine or from a sunny trail into shadows, he wants to wait for his eyes to get used to the change. Remember that when you're leading a horse out of the barn or riding in the sunshine.

Like other animals with long dish-shaped ears, horses have very good hearing. They find sounds by turning one or both ears in any direction. When you're leading or riding a horse, you'll often see that he can hear something long before you do.

A horse often shows what he's thinking by what he does with his ears. For example, a horse that's unhappy will lay his ears back against his head.

Take it from Two Bits, our sense of smell is as sharp as our hearing. The moment a horse picks up an unfamiliar smell, he tries to see whether it's coming from a friend or an enemy.

How many teeth a horse has depends on whether the horse is a "she" or a "he." A full-grown mare has thirty-six teeth. A stallion or a gelding has forty. The four extras are called tushes.

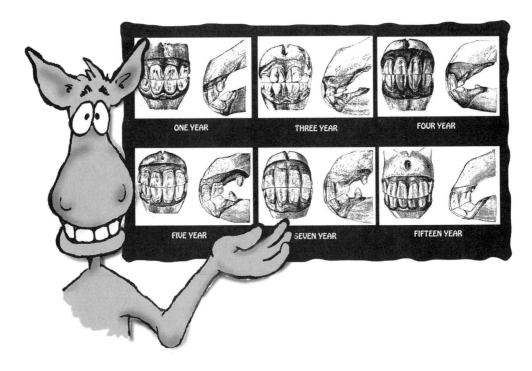

ONE YEAR   THREE YEAR   FOUR YEAR
FIVE YEAR   SEVEN YEAR   FIFTEEN YEAR

The front teeth bite off grass and hay, while the back teeth grind the food.

You didn't get all your teeth at once. Neither do horses. Teeth come in at different ages, and some teeth change their shape over time. That's how you're able to tell how old a horse is when looking at his teeth. Ask someone who knows about horses to show you how it's done.

Horses are able to feel even the lighest touch to their skin. We'll bite or kick at even tiny bugs that buzz around or land on us. That's why you need to be careful whenever you're around a horse. You don't want to be standing too close when a horse decides to kick at a bug that's bothering him.

THE COLORS OF THE HORSE

Horses come in many colors. American Quarter Horses come in thirteen of them. There's a picture of them on page one of the color insert.

The colors are:

bay: a brown body with a black mane and tail, often with black lower legs.

black: all-black body, mane, and tail.

blue roan: a mixture of white and black hairs that gives the color blue.

brown: a brown or black body with light areas at the nose, eyes, and inside the upper legs. The mane and tail are black.

chestnut: a dark red-brown body, mane, and tail.

sorrel: a red-brown body, mane, and tail. Because chestnut and sorrel colors are so close, people sometimes confuse the names, with Western riders using "sorrel" to describe both colors, and English-style riders using "chestnut."

dun: a yellow or gold body, with a black or brown mane and tail. There is a dark stripe that runs along the horse's back and dark stripes on his legs. Red dun is a yellow body with a red mane and tail.

buckskin: the same color as a dun but without the stripe down the back.

gray: a mixture of white with any other dark-colored hair that gives the color gray.

grullo: a gray body color like the color of a mouse, with black mane and tail. There is usually a black stripe that runs down the horse's back.

palomino: a golden yellow coat with white mane and tail.

red roan: a mixture of white with red hairs over most of the horse's body.

Marks

Some horses have white marks on their face. These marks are:

bald face: a very wide blaze that can go around the eyes or the nose or even both.

blaze: a mark that runs the length of the face.

snip: a mark between the nostrils.

star: a small mark on the forehead.

strip: a narrow mark between the forehead and nostrils.

Some horses have white marks on their legs. American Quarter Horses can have four types:

coronet: a mark all the way around the leg above the hoof.

pastern/half pastern: a marking around the pastern.

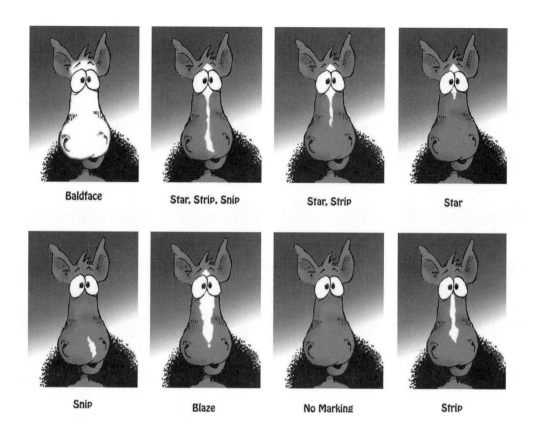

| Baldface | Star, Strip, Snip | Star, Strip | Star |

| Snip | Blaze | No Marking | Strip |

sock: a mark that goes from the hoof halfway to the knee or the hock.

stocking: a mark that goes from the hoof up to the knee or the hock.

HOW DOES A HORSE MOVE?

Humans can walk and run and hop and skip and jump. Horses can walk, jog (also called trot), lope (also called canter), and gallop. The kinds of steps that horses take are called gaits. People tell which gait a horse is moving at by watching how his feet hit the ground.

You can learn the gaits by making believe your fingers are the legs of a horse. Put the tips of your thumb, first finger, middle finger, and fourth (ring) finger of your right hand on the top of a desk or table. That's using all your fingers except for your little finger.

Put your first finger in front of your thumb and your middle finger in front of your fourth finger. That will make your thumb the horse's left hind leg. Your first finger becomes the horse's left front leg. Your middle finger is his right front leg, and your fourth finger is his right hind leg.

Got that?

A horse's walk has four beats. Each foot hits the ground one at a time, even when the horse is walking fast.

To walk your "horse fingers," take a step forward with your thumb. Now take one with your first finger. Take one with your fourth finger. Then one with your middle finger.

That's how a horse walks: He starts with his left hind leg, then moves his left front leg, his right hind leg, and his right foreleg.

Keep going until your horse walks across the desk or the table. And please don't forget to stop when you get to the edge!

The jog, or trot, has two beats because the horse's feet hit the ground two at a time. Are you ready to trot?

Take a step with your thumb and your middle finger at the same time. Then move your first finger and your fourth finger together. That's all it takes to trot: left hind leg and right front leg, then left front leg and right hind leg.

The Natural Gaits of the American Quarter Horse

walk   trot   canter   gallop

The lope, or canter, has three beats. The order in which the feet hit the ground depends on whether the horse is on his right or his left lead (say the word as if it's written "leed").

Let's start with a lope on the left lead. Start by moving your fourth finger. Next move your thumb and middle finger at the same time. Then move your first finger. That's the right hind leg, the left hind and right front legs together, then the left front leg.

To make your "finger horse" lope on his right lead, start with your thumb, then move your first and fourth fingers together, then your middle finger.

WHY DOES A HORSE BEHAVE LIKE A HORSE?

A good way to understand horses is to learn why they behave the way they do.

Take it from Professor Two Bits, the single most important thing any horse cares about is being safe. We've spent millions of years worrying about other animals that wanted to eat us. That's something a horse just can't seem to forget. Whenever something scares us, we try to get away from whatever it might be. Once we're far enough away, then and only then do we stop and think about whether there was a real cause to be frightened.

In other words, first we run, then we ask questions.

Horses need to be able to hear danger as well as see it. Anything that gets in the way of being able to hear things, like thunder or other loud noises, makes us nervous.

Horses like to be with other horses. We feel safer being in a herd, which is the word for a group of horses. You can see how much horses like to be in a herd when you're out riding with other people. If you try to ride your horse away from the others, he may not want to leave. He may look back and "talk" as if to say, "I want to stay with my friends."

A group of horses is called a herd. Staying in a herd makes horses feel safe while they enjoy the company of their friends. (The Quarter Horse Journal)

Even though horses like to be in herds, we're not always good friends with every other horse. Especially not at first. Just like a new kid in the neighborhood, a horse that's new must learn to fit in. That's true even if the herd consists of just one other horse.

Even horses that know each other can become unhappy when another horse comes too close in a field or on a trail ride. Riders and other people around horses must learn to watch out for two horses that don't like being close to each other. They'll put their ears back and sometimes try to bite. If you're riding, you should move your horse away. If you're on the ground, you'll want to get out of the way.

But horses can also be very friendly toward each other. One way we show our feelings is to rub each other with our noses and blow into each other's noses.

Just the way horses like to be in a herd, we also like to be at home. Home means a safe place with food and a barn or a pasture of our own.

When we're away from home, we can't wait to get back. You can see that for yourself when you're on a trail ride. Just see how horses try to move faster when they know they're heading home.

Just like humans, horses are different. Some are friendly and like being around people (that's me!). Others don't much care. Some horses are curious. Some like to have fun by trying to get out of their barn or pasture or even tearing their blankets into pieces.

But other horses are never bored and don't get into trouble. As I said, we're all different.

Horses aren't very good at hiding their feelings. We show how we feel by what's called body language. A horse that opens his eyes wide or lays back his ears or curls his lips to show his teeth or lifts a hind foot is telling you he's getting upset or that he's already mad.

A horse that's nervous or scared will snort, open his eyes wide, and make his body tense (you humans do that too, don't you?). A curious horse opens his eyes and puts his ears forward.

A tired horse keeps his eyes half-closed. His ears and lower lip will droop. That body language may also tell you he's already sound asleep.

Do horses talk? Sort of, but not in words (except for me, of course!). The sounds that horses make and when and where they make them are all clues to what they're trying to say. A lonely horse will whinny (some people use the word "neigh," pronounced "nay") to attract the attention of another horse or person. A gentle nicker can be a sign that the horse is waiting for something good to happen—horses nicker when a barn's feed cart starts making its dinnertime rounds.

Can horses sense human emotions? Sometimes better than you think. That's especially true when it comes to fear. All animals—including humans—give off a special odor when they're frightened, a "smell of fear" that animals with good senses of smell are quick to pick up. When some horses catch that smell from a person, they try to take advantage by not going near the person or doing what the person wants them to do.

You say you don't want that to happen to you? Then just act calmly and confidently around a horse, and he'll listen to you all day.

HOW DO HORSES LEARN?

Horses learn by a process called conditioning. That involves being taught to do something every time the horse is asked to do it. It's learning by repeating.

For example, if you want your horse to move forward, you relax your reins and press against his sides with both your legs. If he moves sideways or backward or doesn't move at all, you keep pressing until he moves forward. And after several times, the horse comes to learn that your leg pressure is the signal to move forward.

We horses also learn on our own through experience. For example, brushing against an electric fence teaches a horse to stay away from the fence. We're good at learning not to repeat mistakes because we have an excellent memory. Even months after a horse is startled by a deer on a trail, passing that place again may still make him jumpy.

As good as our memory may be for some things, horses can connect being punished with having done something wrong only if the correction comes immediately after the wrongdoing. Even a few moments after the horse misbehaves, the connection will be lost forever. If the horse is punished then, he feels he's being treated unfairly. And who can blame him?

Each and every time you handle or ride a horse, you're training him. That's why you need to be consistent, to do the same things the same way. We horses are creatures of habit. We don't like change or surprises. For example, if you clean your horse's feet in the same order every time, he'll expect his feet to be handled in that order. But if you don't, if you start by picking up a different foot than you did the last time, you'll confuse him.

Everything to do with handling a horse comes down to understanding and communication. Successful partnerships work when everyone "speaks" the same language. And that's never truer than in the partnership between you and your horse.

2

MEET THE
AMERICAN QUARTER
HORSE

Now let's learn about the American Quarter Horse.

Once upon a time, and I mean hundreds of millions of years ago, horses lived in North America. Nowhere else in the world, just North America. They didn't look at all like the horses that live today. These horses were no bigger than large dogs, and instead of a hard hoof, they had three toes on each foot.

But over the years these horses grew in size until they were about as big as small ponies. Their toes also changed into the hard hooves that horses now have on their feet.

A few million years ago, North America became too cold for horses to live in comfort. They traveled north and west, across a piece of land that used to join together Alaska and Asia.

When the horses reached Asia, they split up into two groups. One group stayed in the northern parts of Asia and Europe. They grew long hair to protect against the cold. They also grew in

size, becoming tall and strong enough to pull heavy wagons and to carry knights who wore heavy metal suits called armor.

The other group of horses traveled south. They found a home in the warmer weather of Arabia and North Africa. They grew lighter in build and faster in speed than their northern cousins. This was the type of horse that explorers brought to America with them, starting with Columbus's second trip in 1493.

Another man who brought horses was the Spanish explorer Cortés, who started cattle ranching in Mexico around the year 1530. The lighter and faster horses he brought were very good at this work because vaqueros (which is the Spanish word for cowboys) needed horses that could move fast to keep up with the cows.

The kind of lives that horses led in the early days of the American West depended on where they lived. Some herded cattle on big ranches in Texas and California. Others were ridden by Native Americans. A third group escaped from their owners and became wild horses called mustangs. Nobody owned or rode these horses.

All horses had one thing in common. They were strong and tough. They could go for hours and hours at a time and over the hardest ground without becoming tired or sore.

Our story now moves east. People who lived in Virginia and the Carolinas in the 1700s, around the time of the Revolutionary War, had horses that pulled plows and wagons. But sometimes the people liked to hold races to see whose horse was the fastest. They called these contests "short racing" because the races were held at a distance of a quarter of a mile.

There were several reasons why they chose that distance. Races could be held only on flat land that had no trees. That usu-

ally meant using a road, and the roads of those days seldom had flat and wide stretches that were longer than a quarter mile.

Then too, the horses had farming and other hard work to do. Their owners didn't want them using up all their strength racing more than a quarter of a mile.

People began calling these horses Quarter Running Horses.

There were longer races too. They were run by Thoroughbreds, another kind of horse that came from Europe. Thoroughbreds could run not only fast but for up to three or four miles at a time.

Thoroughbreds have long legs and thin bodies, but one stallion in Virginia looked like no other Thoroughbred. He had a very strong body with a wide chest and back. He was also a very fast runner at short distances. His name was Janus, and all his children were able to run a quarter of a mile very fast.

The Quarter Running Horse was a favorite of the settlers who moved to the Midwest and Southwest starting in the 1830s. One of the most famous horses was Steel Dust. Steel Dust was about fifteen hands high and was described as looking like a

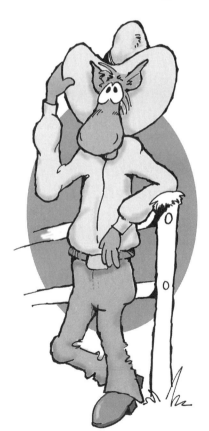

Thoroughbred, but shorter and wider.

Steel Dust's sons and daughters could run just as fast as he could. As more and more people heard about them, they and other Quarter Runners became known as "Steeldusts."

Settlers and ranchers liked these horses for more than just racing. Their speed made them good at helping to move cows around pastures or along a trail. This is known as working cattle.

These horses were smart too. They seemed to know what cattle would do or

where they would try to run off to almost before the cattle themselves did. Cowboys called it having "cow sense."

All these things made Steeldust horses perfect for all kinds of cutting, roping, and other types of ranch work.

Ranch owners worked at making the perfect cow horse, strong enough to work a 1,000-pound steer, fast enough to chase after a runaway cow, and able to change directions very quickly. Cowboys didn't want horses that were very tall, because the cowboys had to get on and off them easily.

That's why most Steeldust cow horses weighed anywhere from 950 to 1,150 pounds and were about fifteen hands high. Most of them were one solid color, such as sorrel or bay.

You'll learn more about the history of the American Quarter Horse at the end of this book when we learn about an organization called the American Quarter Horse Association.

FOR FURTHER INFORMATION:

The Quarter Horse Journal and *The Quarter Racing Journal*, both published monthly, and *America's Horse*, published every other month, report on current events and other features. Membership in AQHA includes a subscription to *America's Horse*. You can also purchase a subscription to *The Quarter Horse Journal* and *The Quarter Racing Journal*.

Two books contain more on the start of the breed and AQHA: *They Rode Good Horses: The First Fifty Years of the American Quarter Horse Association* by Don Hedgpeth (published by AQHA) covers the Association up to 1990.

The Colonial Quarter Race Horse by Alexander Mackay-Smith (published by Colonial Quarter Horse Publication) tells about the early years of America's racing history.

AQHA offers the following videos:

On the Fifth Day: This video gives the history of horses from the beginning to when the American Quarter Horse started in America. Also available in Spanish. 28 minutes.

The Horse and Society: Learn how people and horses have been helping each other as long as they have been together. 59 minutes.

All in a Day's Ride: Learn about the life of a cowboy and how American Quarter Horses work on America's ranches. 25 minutes.

3

TIPS ON
RIDING YOUR
AMERICAN QUARTER
HORSE

Let me explain what I mean by "riding *your* American Quarter Horse," even if you don't own one now.

Before you even think about getting a horse of your own, you'll want to learn how to ride. Riding is the best way to enjoy horses and to learn about them.

You don't need to own a horse to learn to ride. Maybe you're taking lessons now. And because the American Quarter Horse is the world's most popular breed, you may be riding one. That's why, whenever you're on the horse, you can think of him as *your* American Quarter Horse.

This book isn't meant to be a how-to-ride book. No one ever learned to ride a horse just by reading a book. Learning to ride takes a real live teacher. And while that person is teaching you, he or she can make sure that both you and your horse are safe and comfortable.

Your teacher may be someone in your family, an older friend, or perhaps someone who teaches riding for a living. Your folks can help you decide who would be a good teacher for you.

But books can be helpful. They can explain many important things about horses and how to handle them and how to ride them. That's why I want to be your teacher now and share a few ideas with you.

Wearing the right clothing makes riding easier and safer. Your shoes or boots must have heels. Heels keep your feet from sliding through the stirrups.

Many riders wear a helmet for riding. A helmet is another name for a hard hat. These people feel that a helmet protects their head in case of an accident, just like people who wear helmets

(*AQHA photo by Wyatt McSpadden*)

when riding a bike or taking part in other sports. Whether to wear a helmet is up to you, your folks, and the people who own the horse that you ride. But if you do wear a helmet, it should have a chin strap. The helmet and the strap must fit properly.

The first time you get on a horse, you'll be taught to do so from the horse's left side. You get off a horse from the left side too. Most horses wouldn't really mind you getting on or off from the right side. In fact, cowboys who rope cows often get off that way. Still, horses are used to people getting on and off from the left, so that's the way to do it.

Here's an easy way to remember: *The left side is the right side, and the right side is the wrong side!*

As you get on your horse, get into the saddle slowly. Letting yourself drop down like a big sack of potatoes hurts a horse's back, and that's not a very pleasant way to begin a ride.

Practice putting your feet in the stirrups without looking down. Instead of swinging your whole foot, poke with your toes to find the stirrups. Then slide your feet into them. Practice this while your horse is standing still. Then practice while he's walking.

Good riders can kick their feet out of their stirrups, then put them back in at the walk, the trot, and even the canter.

The belt that holds the saddle in place is called the cinch. Sometimes it's called the girth. You may have to check several times during a ride to make sure the cinch or girth is tight enough. Some horses like to puff up their bellies when the saddle is put on. Then when they let the air out, the cinch or girth gets loose. If it's too loose, the saddle can slip.

Your teacher will show you how to tighten the cinch or girth. He or she may want to tighten it for you.

Some horses like to puff up their bellies when the rider tightens the girth.

You ask a horse to move by squeezing your legs against his sides. Horses have been trained to move forward when they feel a rider's legs there.

That's why your legs should hang straight down your horse's sides. An easy way to tell they're in the right place is to stand in the stirrups. Try it while your horse is standing still or walking slowly. If you feel yourself falling forward toward the horse's neck, your legs are too far back. If you feeling yourself fall backward, your legs are too far forward. If you can stand, your legs are where they belong.

When you're able to stand in your stirrups, sit back down in the saddle. Keep your legs where they were when you stood up. That's where they should be when you ride.

Another way to tell if your feet are too far forward is to look down. If you can see your toes, move your feet back behind your knees.

Think of riding as having a conversation with your horse. You speak to your horse by using your hands on the reins and your legs against his sides.

You can also use your voice. Making a clicking sound will tell your horse to move forward. Saying "whoa" (which sounds like "ho!") tells him to slow down or stop.

Your horse answers through the way he responds to your cues.

Nobody likes a conversation when someone is shouting. Horses don't like it either. A hard kick in your horse's belly to tell him to move forward is like shouting. A squeeze with your lower leg is the right way to ask.

Yanking hard on the reins to tell your horse to stop is like shouting. Squeezing the reins with gentle pressure is asking.

Riding a horse is a matter of balance, like staying on in-line skates or a skateboard. You don't need to

This young Western rider is sitting tall in the saddle, relaxed but ready to ask her horse to move forward. (The Quarter Horse Journal)

use your strength to stay in the saddle. Wrapping your legs around your horse's belly will only squeeze you out of the saddle.

There's another reason not to squeeze too hard. Squeezing hard is the signal to move faster. Horses are taught to move away from pressure. Squeeze very hard and your horse may go faster than you really want him to go.

Where you look is very important. When you look to the right or to the left, you turn your head in that direction. Then the rest of your body turns that way too. Turning your body helps tell your horse to go left or right, just the way pulling on the reins tells him.

Keep your eyes looking up and ahead. Looking down makes you lean forward. Leaning forward makes you lose your balance.

Trotting can be bouncy if you try to sit. But trotting feels more comfortable when you lift yourself out of the saddle, then sink back down at each trotting step the horse takes. That's called posting. English-style riders and some Western riders post the trot.

Posting may look like hard work—going up-down up-down up-down—but it doesn't take strength. Instead, the way your horse trots pushes you up and out of the saddle. Then you sink back into the saddle at your horse's next step.

You don't need to post very high. Just get your seat out of the saddle.

And please don't lean on the reins to hang on. You should post from your legs and not from your hands.

If you feel yourself losing your balance, reach for your horse's mane and grab a handful. That's a good way to hold on in case you find yourself slipping. Don't drop your reins if you can help it.

At the end of every lesson, remember to thank your teacher. Then thank your other teacher too. That's your horse. Giving him an apple or a carrot after you've gotten off is a terrific thank-you present.

OUT ON THE TRAIL

There will come a time in your riding lessons when your teacher will say, "You now ride well enough to go out for a trail ride." That's the day that every new rider looks forward to.

But just because you can leave the ring doesn't mean you should go out on the trail all by yourself. Your instructor or another older rider should go along with you. Maybe some other riders will go along too. That's good. Riding with other people is more fun than going out by yourself. It's also safer.

Like with riding a bike or driving a car on the street, there are rules that you must follow when you ride a horse on the trail. Here's what you need to know.

RULES OF THE ROAD

Listen to the leader. The older person who takes you out on the trail is the leader. Having a nice and a safe ride depends on listening to what he or she tells you at all times.

Ride only where you're welcome. Not everyone wants people riding over their land. Stay off land that has signs that say you shouldn't ride there.

Stay on the trail. A riding trail is a safe place for horses to be. Other places may have holes in the ground, broken glass, or other things that can hurt your horse. That's why you should stay on the trail.

Ride one behind another. Ride side by side only when the trail is wide enough. Otherwise, stay one behind another.

Some horses like to be at the front of a group. Others are happier when they're in back. Your trail leader will help figure out which horse should go in front of another.

Stay at least one horse length behind the horse in front of you. Getting too close to the horse ahead of you can make both your horse and the horse in front nervous.

If you get to a steep hill, stay two horse lengths apart going uphill and three horse lengths apart when going downhill. Staying that far apart keeps horses from bumping into one another if one of them starts to slip or slide down the hill.

If you must pass the horse in front of you, wait until the trail is wide enough so that you won't get too close.

Pick a good gait. You'll spend most of your trail ride walking, but a jog trot is fun too. So is a lope, but only if all the riders in the group know how to lope.

When you decide to move at a faster gait, make sure everyone in the group knows it before you start. That way you'll all have plenty of time to get ready.

Check your cinch or girth. Remember that some horses puff up their bellies when their saddle is first put on. You may need to make your cinch or girth tighter during your trail ride. If it stays loose, the saddle might slip.

If one person needs to tighten the saddle cinch, everyone else should stop and wait until it's done.

Don't hold tree branches. Holding a tree branch for the rider behind you may seem like a friendly thing to do. It's not, though. By the time the person behind you gets close enough to reach the branch, it will have snapped back in his or her face. Besides, your horses will have gotten too close to each other. Just push the branch aside for yourself. The riders in front of you and behind you will do the same.

Hold gates open. Whoever opens a gate should hold it open until everyone has passed through. Then, if the person needs to get down to shut the gate, wait until he or she gets back on the horse before you move off.

Make sure all gates are closed. Letting cows or other animals get out of the field may make the owner of the land stop letting people ride there.

Keep the land neat. Leaving garbage along the trail is another way to make owners of riding land unhappy. It's also bad manners (like leaving garbage anywhere else).

Be aware of others on the trail. You may share some trails with hikers and bike riders, as well as other horseback riders. Stay on the right side of the trail, the way cars drive on the right side of the road. That way, you won't bump into people coming toward you.

Two riders should pass each other at the slower gait. If you're trotting and the other rider is walking, it's up to you to slow down to the walk.

Walk past a hiker or biker. Then don't go any faster until you're far beyond the person on foot.

Be careful around corners. Slow down around corners you can't see around. You never know when someone is coming the other way. They can't see you either.

Make sure people know you're there. People on foot or on bikes may be talking to each other or listening to a Walkman. If they look as if they don't see you, call out to them or wave your hand so they know you're there too.

Be smart about traffic. Some trails go across roads. Others go beside roads. Not all drivers of cars and trucks slow down when they see horses.

To tell drivers to slow down, hold out your hand and pat it down a few times, as if you are dribbling a basketball. Then, when the car or truck slows down or stops, thank the driver by smiling and waving.

To eat or not to eat? Should you let your horse stop and eat during a trail ride? Sometimes it's hard to keep him from grabbing a bite of leaves from a tree. But letting him stop and eat grass isn't always a good idea. If you let him do it once, you're giving him the idea that he can do it anytime and anywhere.

This is something to talk about with your trail leader.

Warm up and cool down. Good riders care about their horses every step of the way. They give their horses the chance to warm up and then cool off. How? By walking the first mile away from the barn and walking the last mile home.

FOR FURTHER INFORMATION:

The AQHA affiliate in your state, province, or country can tell you about trail riding. And if your family is thinking about a riding trip somewhere else, get in touch with the AQHA affiliate wherever you're going.

4

BEFORE YOU GET YOUR AMERICAN QUARTER HORSE

Let's say you've been taking riding lessons for a while now. You may be learning at a local stable, or someone who owns a horse is teaching you.

And when you're not riding, you read books and magazines about horses. You watch AQHA's show *America's Horse* whenever it's on TV. You go to horse shows and you watch American Quarter Horse racing whenever you get the chance.

Yes, one thing's for sure: You love horses and you love to ride. But you think one thing is missing. You don't have an American Quarter Horse of your very own.

But don't start telling your folks what you want for your birthday or write letters to Santa Claus just yet. Let's first make sure that owning a horse, and especially one that you would keep at home, is a good idea.

You can take it from me, Two Bits, when I say that anyone who owns a horse must be able to take care of him. Horses aren't gold-fish or dogs or cats. You don't keep them in a fishbowl or let them sleep on the floor next to your bed. You don't walk them around the block twice a day or change their litter box once a week. If you're going away from home for a while, you can't leave them with a bowl of dry food.

A horse must be fed and cleaned and exercised every day. His stall and pasture need to be cleaned too. It doesn't matter if it's raining or snowing or if there's something else you'd rather be doing. These chores come first.

Someone your age may be able to clean a stall or take a horse out to the pasture, but other things to do with owning a horse need an older person to do them. Like buying feed and hay. And fixing the barn or the fence when they need to be fixed.

Sure, you can help, but you can't do all the work yourself.

That's why you can't own a horse unless there's a grown-up who'll help. Not just any grown-up, but someone who lives near you and who knows a great deal about horses. It might be a parent or an older brother or older sister. Maybe it's someone who lives near you. Whoever it is, let's call that person your friend, even though it may be someone in your family.

You can still be friends with a family member, right?!

Do you know such a person?

An animal that's as big as a horse needs lots of land to live on. How much land is enough? Probably more than you think. Your backyard may seem big to you, but horses like to nibble on grass and move around all the time. If you don't have enough land, the grass will be gone in no time, and the ground will turn into mud. No horse would want to live there.

The more land you have, the more a horse can move around. That way the grass has a chance to grow back after the horse eats it.

The right kind of land for a horse is a field that can be fenced in. That's called a pasture.

Some pastures have a pond or a stream full of good drinking water. If the pasture on your land has no pond or stream, you can put in a tub and fill it with water, using a hose or buckets. Or you can give your horse water from buckets.

Any weeds or bushes in the pasture can't be bad for a horse to eat.

Fruit trees in a pasture can be a problem. They will drop lots of apples or other treats on the ground. A horse may eat too many, and that will give him a bad stomach-ache.

You'll also need a place to ride. You may want a riding ring, which is sometimes called a corral (kor-AL). If you don't want one or you don't have enough room, you'll need to be near a field or a trail you can ride on.

The best way to tell whether you have the right kind of land is to ask your friend, the expert. Most towns and cities have laws that say where horses can live. These laws have to do with keeping land—and horses—safe and clean. They are called zoning laws. Even though your next-door neighbors have a horse, there may be different zoning laws for your land.

Your friend or your parents should talk to someone who knows about zoning laws. A lawyer or someone who works for your town or city will know.

Owning and keeping a horse costs money.

Your family will have to build or fix up a shed or a barn, a pasture, and maybe a riding ring.

You'll have to buy equipment like brushes and combs for cleaning the horse; and a wheelbarrow, a rake, and a broom for cleaning his stall. You'll also need things like fly spray and buckets.

The horse will need a saddle, bridle, and a saddle blanket or pad. He'll probably also need other tack and clothing.

You'll need boots and a safety helmet. So will anyone else in your family who will be riding the horse.

Then, of course, there is the cost of buying the horse.

These are things you'll buy or pay for only once.

Other things must be bought or paid for as long as you have a horse.

This group of things starts with feed and hay.

The farrier will have to come about once a month to put new shoes on the horse.

The veterinarian, who is often called the vet, will come to give your horse check-ups to keep him healthy. If the horse gets sick, the vet will have to come more often.

I can hear you and your parents asking, "Okay, but what's the whole cost? How much should we expect to spend?"

There's no one answer that works for everyone. For example, the cost of feed and hay varies in different parts of the country.

You and your folks and your friend will need to talk to someone who owns a horse. Not just any horse, but a horse that is used the way you want to use yours. If all you want to do is trail ride, ask people who use their horses just for trail riding. If you'll want to do horse showing, you need to talk to a person who shows.

Make a list as the person goes through all the costs, then add everything up.

OTHER WAYS TO HAVE A HORSE

Don't feel bad if you don't have enough land or if zoning laws won't let you keep a horse at home. Or even if buying and keeping a horse costs more money than your family is able to spend. There are other ways to have a horse.

Many people keep their horses at stables.

You may not have to look for a stable any farther than where you now take your riding lessons. Or maybe your friend knows of a good place that's near where you live.

But that stable may be full and unable to take any new horses. Or it may charge more money than your folks can spend. If that's the case, you've got to look elsewhere.

As you look at a new stable, you and your folks must ask yourselves certain questions. Does the place have the kind of riding you like to do? (Western or English, riding in a ring and trail riding too?) Can you take lessons at times that are good for you? If you're used to riding on rainy or cold days in an indoor arena, does the new place have one?

Your horse will be happy living in a stall that's big and clean. He'll also want a nice big pasture where he can get fresh air and grass. And he'll want to be cared for by people who are friendly and who like being around horses.

The best way to judge a new stable is to spend time there. Watch what goes on. Talk to people who keep their horses there. Take a lesson to see whether you like the teachers. And talk things over with your friend.

LEASING

When you pay a stable for a lesson or a trail ride, you rent that horse. When you rent for a longer time, for a month or longer, it's called a lease.

Many stables lease some of their better horses. That means you would get that horse whenever you ride. It's a lot like owning him.

Sometimes two people can lease the same horse. They must ride the horse at different times, of course.

SHARING A HORSE

Suppose your family doesn't have the land to keep a horse, but you have a friend who does. Or maybe you have enough land and someone else owns a nice horse that needs a new place to live. Or maybe you and someone you know have enough money between you to buy a horse and keep him at a stable.

That's when you and someone else can share a horse. Although sharing may sound like a great idea, you and your parents need to work out certain things with your partner. The two of you must agree on when each of you gets to ride. If both of you will do the stable chores, you need to agree on who will do which jobs. Everybody's parents must agree about money matters.

Writing everything down is always a smart idea. That way, if someone forgets, you and your partner will know who should do which job.

WORKING

You may be able to keep a horse at another person's barn by working there. You can help with feeding, cleaning stalls, grooming, and doing other jobs after school, on weekends, and during vacations.

Many young people have started out working this way to keep a horse. That's just one more way to own an American Quarter Horse of your own.

FOR FURTHER INFORMATION:

The following videos are about owning a horse:

Horse Sense: Basic safety and grooming tips. 26 minutes.

Horse Sense, The Second Year: Training tips. 26 minutes.

Horse Sense III, The Rider: Horse and rider clothing, saddles, bits, safety, saddling and bridling, mounting, dismounting, basic riding, and gaits. An excellent introduction. 33 minutes.

AQHA has several videos about owning an American Quarter Horse:

America's Horse: A look at the American Quarter Horse and why he is America's favorite horse. 28 minutes.

The American Quarter Horse—You'll Always Remember the Ride: The video shows such AQHA events as shows, races, and AQHA programs. 10 minutes.

5

WHERE TO KEEP YOUR AMERICAN QUARTER HORSE

Once you, your folks, and your friend decide you can keep a horse at home, you'll probably be halfway out the door to look for one. Not so fast! You wouldn't want to move to a new place until you were sure it was ready for you to live there. Neither would a horse. That means you must first set up a pasture or a barn (or both) where the horse can live and work and play.

PASTURE

The simplest way to keep a horse at home is called field keeping. In some parts of the country it's called pasture keeping, or pasturing.

You'll need a large pasture that never gets very muddy and that isn't full of rocks. Mud and rocks are bad for a horse's feet.

The pasture needs lots of grass. Horses like to nibble grass all the time. That's called grazing. Land with nothing to graze makes horses bored and unhappy.

If there is no stream or pond with clean drinking water, the pasture will need a trough, tub, or buckets. Water will have to come from a pipe or a hose or from buckets that someone (maybe you) will carry. In parts of the country where winters are so cold that the water turns into ice, someone will have to break holes in a frozen pond or trough, or else carry buckets full of fresh water.

The pasture will need a fence to keep your horse from wandering away. The fence's posts, rails, and gate must be strong enough not to break when a 1,000-pound horse leans against them.

Some people like to use electric fences. The horse feels a little tingle when he leans against it, and he learns to stay away.

A lake or a pond at the edge of the pasture may seem like a good way to keep a horse inside. But horses can wade and swim, and they can walk across a frozen pond in winter. You're much better off with fences all around the pasture.

Trees in a pasture give shade in summer and protect against wind and snow in winter. You should also have a shed. A popular type is a shed with walls on three sides. The fourth side, the one that's open, should face south to keep the horse out of cold north winds. A sloping roof lets rain and melted snow run off.

You can keep feed, hay, and tools in a second shed. That one should have four sides. If it's inside the pasture, the shed will need a door with a strong lock. Otherwise, the horse can break in and get at the feed and hay.

Not all horses like to live alone in a pasture. They get lonely. If that's how you're planning to keep your horse, try to buy one that's used to such a life.

Barns

If you had the choice between standing in an open field in the rain and snow or being nice and warm and dry in a barn, which would you choose? A horse would make the same choice.

It's nice to have food and other items under the same roof as the horse. That's why most people keep their horses in a barn.

A barn belongs on dry, flat land. There should be an easy way to drive a truck up to the building. If not, you'll have to carry heavy sacks of grain and bedding and heavy bales of hay from far away.

If there's no well nearby, water will have to be brought by pipe, hose, or buckets.

Very few barns have only one stall. Bags of bedding, wheelbarrows, and other large items can live in the spare stall. Besides, you never know when another horse may come for a sleepover. Or your family may decide one day to get a second horse!

The ceiling of the barn should be high enough so that your horse won't bump his head, even when he tries to stand up on his hind legs.

A square stall is called a box stall. A box stall for an American Quarter Horse should be at least twelve feet square. It should have a window so that your horse can look out and fresh air can come in.

Metal bars on the top half of the inside wall and the door let a horse look out. You can have a good look inside too.

Although cement makes a strong floor for the rest of the barn, it's not the best choice for a stall. Cement is slippery when it's dry and even more slippery when wet. Besides, standing on hard cement can hurt your horse's feet and legs.

Wooden floors are more comfortable, but plain soil or clay can soak up wetness better than wood can.

The stall should have a feed bin on the wall for grain. For drinking, some owners like to use a water fountain that fills up again whenever the water gets too low. However, many people prefer to use water buckets. That way, they can tell how much their horse has drunk. That's important to know, because a horse that doesn't drink enough water may not be feeling well.

If you use buckets, two strong ones hung from hooks on the wall can be filled using a hose.

Saddles, bridles, grooming tools, and everything else your horse will need can be kept in a separate room called a tack room. The tack room will need racks to hold the saddle and bridle. It should also have many shelves. A sink with hot and cold water is very useful. So is electricity for lights and tools.

A separate room to store feed and bedding means you won't always have bales of hay and sacks of grain in the way. The room must have a cement floor and walls to keep out mice and other small animals that like to eat grain.

Grain and other feed are stored in metal or thick plastic cans that small animals can't get into.

The top floor of many barns is used to store hay, but only if the floor is strong enough to hold many thousands of pounds of hay bales.

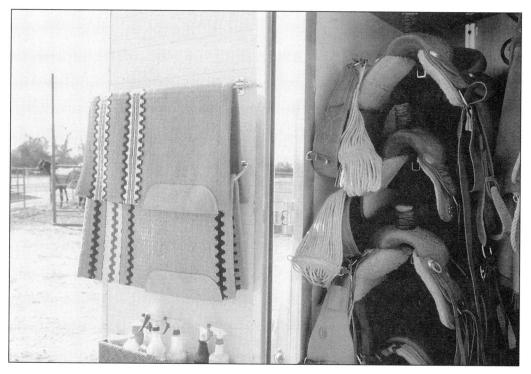

Saddles and other tack will stay in good shape—and not get lost—if you hang them in the tack room where they belong. (Greg Thon/Cowboy Tack)

Your land may already have a barn or a shed, but that doesn't always mean it's ready for a horse to live in. The floor or walls may be falling apart. Sometimes the barn can be fixed up, but other times pulling it down and starting over is a better idea. Your folks and your friend will decide which is better.

An empty garage can sometimes be turned into a barn, but not a garage where your family keeps a car. It is as dangerous for horses to breathe gas as it is for people. Never keep a car and a horse in the same building.

There are many ways to build a small horse barn. You and your folks can learn a great deal from books and magazines. Your friend or someone at a tack shop, bookstore, or library can help you find good ones. Also look at barns near where you live. There are companies that build barns. You can find them in horse magazines. Someone from the company will be happy to talk to you and your folks about what you'll need.

Manure Pile

A healthy horse makes about ten pounds of manure every day. That's seventy pounds every week. In addition to manure, dirty stall bedding must be put someplace before there's enough to take away.

Manure and dirty bedding attract flies and other bugs. They also have a smell that not everyone likes. That's why your manure pile can't be too close to the barn or to anyone's house.

Either someone will come to get the manure or a grown-up in your family will have to drive it away. That's why the pile should also be easy for a truck to get to.

Riding Ring or Arena

Not every horse owner needs a ring to ride in. But even if you enjoy trail riding, there will be days when you'll want to ride at home, and a ring will come in handy. For example, you don't want to be caught out on the trail if it rains.

A ring is also handy if you're taking lessons or training for horse shows.

A ring should be built on flat and dry ground that doesn't have too many rocks.

A fence around the ring keeps a horse's mind on his job. Boards or pipes make good fences. The gate should be wide enough so that both you and your horse can go through side by side.

After your horse goes around and around a lot, his feet will make holes and ruts in the ground. When that happens, you'll have to fill in the holes and smooth out the dirt. Some people use a tractor for this chore, while other people use a shovel and a rake.

6

CHOOSING YOUR AMERICAN QUARTER HORSE

Of all the wonderful American Quarter Horses in the world, which one will be the right one for you?

To answer that question, you must rely on your friend, that older person who knows all about horses, to help you. Your friend will know that someone your age and with your riding experience needs a special horse. You need a kind and gentle animal that's as easy to care for as he is easy to ride.

Even before you and your friend start looking for a horse, you should learn what to look for. That means looking at horses in a way you probably never looked at them before.

You'll also have some homework to do. Study the picture on page 4 and learn the names of the parts of a horse. That way, you'll know exactly what your friend means when he or she talks about a gaskin or a stifle.

Then go along with your friend to look at a real live American Quarter Horse. Maybe it's a horse your friend owns, or it might be the horse you ride now.

Make believe you're looking at the horse for the very first time. Stand back and look at the whole horse. Study the way he's built.

Conformation means how close a horse comes to being perfect. You may know that idea from halter classes at horse shows. A horse that has good conformation looks balanced. His parts should match. For example, one leg shouldn't be thicker or thinner than another, and his head shouldn't look too big for his body.*

Ask your friend questions. And listen to your friend explain how that horse is put together. That means the way the horse is built.

You won't learn everything about horses by looking at just one horse this way, or even by looking at a few horses. But it's a good start, especially when your friend explains what to look for.

Your friend will also talk to you about what's a good age for your first horse. Like puppies and kittens, very young horses are very cute. But they need to grow up and be trained before they are safe to ride. You'll want a horse that's no younger than seven or eight years old, but he should probably be even older.

Knowing what you want to do with your horse will also help you find the horse for you. If you plan to do barrel racing or hunt-seat equitation, you'll want a horse that has that kind of training. That's another reason why buying an older horse is a good idea.

You've learned from the horses you've ridden that they come in different sizes and shapes. Some are taller than others. Some are skinny, some are round.

---

*To learn more about conformation, look at the AQHA booklet *A Guide to Buying American Quarter Horses.* Another good booklet is *Conformation: The Relationship of Form to Function* by Dr. Marvin Beeman, also available from AQHA.

People come in different sizes and shapes too. If you're small for your age, you won't want a very big horse. If you're tall, a small horse won't fit you very well.

Okay, now let's start looking for an American Quarter Horse for you.

WHERE TO LOOK

One good place to start looking would be the stable where you're taking lessons or going on trail rides. People there, and especially your teacher, will know the kind of horse that's good for you. If there's no such horse for sale at the stable, those people can ask around.

The American Quarter Horse Association has a free service that gives the names and addresses of people in your area who can help you find a horse. Your parents can get these names by phoning AQHA.

In addition, you and your folks can ask veterinarians, farriers, and tack-store owners. Look for ads in newspapers and magazines (including *The Quarter Horse Journal* and *The Quarter Racing Journal*). There are even Web sites where you can find American Quarter Horses for sale.

At the same time, your friend will be talking to people he or she knows.

TRYING OUT A HORSE

One day your friend will tell you about a horse that he or she has heard of. It's one you should try. Your parents or your friend will set up a time to see the horse, and you count the hours till it's time to go.

Let's make believe that the horse's owner is a woman who sells horses for a living. She's waiting for you and your friend at the door to her barn. You look inside and see a nice clean stable. That's good, because people who keep their barns neat and clean usually take good care of their horses.

You and your friend follow the owner out to the pasture. The horse is waiting. He's a sorrel American Quarter Horse that the owner says is thirteen years old. His name is Star.

Star seems happy to see his owner. That's good too, because you'll want a horse that likes people and is easy to catch.

While Star's owner leads him up to the barn, you and your friend look at how he is is built and how he moves.

You also watch how Star likes to be handled. You see that he leads easily and stands quietly when his owner starts to clean him.

Your friend will run a hand down Star's legs. If your friend finds any bumps, he or she will ask the owner how Star got them.

Your friend will also look at Star's teeth to make sure the horse is truly the age the owner thinks he is.

Star doesn't seem to mind being saddled and bridled. You watch excitedly because you can't wait to get on and ride him.

But that won't happen right away. The owner or another rider always gets on first. That's safer, in case the horse does something silly. Also, people on the ground have a better view of how a horse moves, and that's what you want to see.

So you and your friend walk down to the riding ring and watch the owner ride Star. She asks him to walk, jog, and lope. First they go one way around the ring, then the other way.

As you watch, you look to see whether Star has nice easy gaits, whether he steers easily, and whether he looks happy to be ridden. For example, if he keeps his ears pointed forward most of the time, you'll know he's a happy horse.

If you and your friend like what you see so far, the owner will get off Star and help you get on. You sit quietly while the stirrups are set for you, then you start to ride.

Your job is to ride the horse as well as you can. You should also ask yourself certain questions while you ride. Does Star listen to your signals? Are his walk, jog, and lope comfortable? When you get to the end of the ring, does he turn easily? Does he lope easily on both leads? When you stop, does he stand quietly?

You shouldn't ride Star any longer than it takes to answer these questions. It's not fair to make him tired, especially when other people may be coming to look at him later that day.

So you get off and hand Star's reins to the owner. And you thank her for the chance to ride him.

Now you and your friend walk a little way off and talk about Star.

Very often, people who are looking for their first horse fall in love with the first horse they try. That's natural. You can't wait to own a horse and Star looks like a good guy. So why not buy him?

Maybe that's a good idea. But maybe it isn't. That's where your friend will be very helpful. People who know a lot about horses can tell whether the first one you try will be right for you.

If your friend doesn't think Star is right for you, please don't be upset. The world is full of nice American Quarter Horses. Just keep looking. And take it from Two Bits, you'll find one that's right for you.

But what if you like Star and your friend likes him too? If the price that the owner asks is what your parents want to spend, there is one more thing to do before Star is yours.*

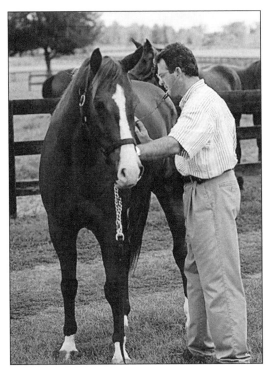

Before you agree to buy a horse, an animal doctor called a veterinarian should make sure the horse is in good health. (Bayer Corporation)

VETERINARY EXAM

You want to make sure you buy a healthy horse. That's why a veterinarian, or vet, should examine Star. Maybe there's a health problem that his owner didn't know about.

How do you find a vet? Not just any animal doctor will do. You need one who knows about horses. Your friend may know such a doctor. Or maybe you can use the vet who cares for the horse you've been learning to ride on.**

---

*Sometimes people who have a horse will give him away. That's usually because the horse has become too old for what the owner wants to do with him. The owner wants to make sure he goes to a good home.

But even though you would save money by taking a "giveaway," you should make sure the horse is the right one for you before you and your folks think about taking him. Once again, your friend will be the best judge of that.

**Another way to find a veterinarian is for your parents to phone the American Association of Equine Practitioners at 1-800-GET-ADVM. They will give you the name of a vet who lives near you.

If the vet says Star is healthy, then you have yourself an American Quarter Horse!

REGISTRATION

An AQHA registration certificate is an important piece of paper. It proves that the horse you bought is an American Quarter Horse. It also means that you and your horse can take part in many American Quarter Horse Association events.

The person who sold you an American Quarter Horse will give you the certificate. Your parents or your friend will make sure the certificate is correct.

When you and your parents tell AQHA that Star has a new owner, AQHA will send you a new paper with your name on it.

That's when you'll know you really own your American Quarter Horse!

FOR FURTHER INFORMATION:

The AQHA offers the following videos on choosing an American Quarter Horse:

Survival of the Fittest: A vet talks about American Quarter Horse conformation. Two parts. Also available in Spanish. 26 minutes each.

Form to Function—The Importance of Conformation: How good conformation helps a horse do his job. 11 minutes.

7

OUTFITTING YOUR AMERICAN QUARTER HORSE

Hi, it's Two Bits, the clothes horse.

People who learn to ride use the saddle and bridle that go with the horse they learn on. The saddle and bridle belong to the horse's owner or the place where the people take lessons.

But when you own your own horse, you'll need your own tack. "Tack" is the word for all the things that horses wear.

Okay, let's find out what you and your horse will need. We'll start with Western tack.

WESTERN TACK

SADDLES

The Western saddle is also known as the stock saddle. It came from the kind of saddle that Spanish soldiers brought to North America over 500 years ago. The soldiers needed to sit tight in their saddles so they wouldn't fall off during a fight. That's why their saddles had a high pommel (POM-el) at the front and a high cantle (CAN-til) at the back.

Cowboys also needed a tight fit. That helped keep them on their horses when the horses made fast starts and stops and quick twists and turns while they chased after cattle.

When cowboys learned to use a rope to catch steers and cows, they needed someplace to tie the end of the rope. That's the reason for the saddle horn.

The frame of a saddle is called the tree. It's made of wood or metal and is covered with heavy leather. Trees come in several styles. A very popular one fits the wide back and flat withers of the American Quarter Horse.

The tree is made up of four parts: the fork, the horn, the bars, and the cantle. The picture on this page shows where they are on the saddle.

The horn is made of wood or metal and is covered with leather. It can be as short as two inches or as tall as four inches. Taller and thicker horns are better for tying ropes to.

The cantle is shaped like a deep dish. It's covered with thick leather, so it's comfortable to sit in for many hours of riding.

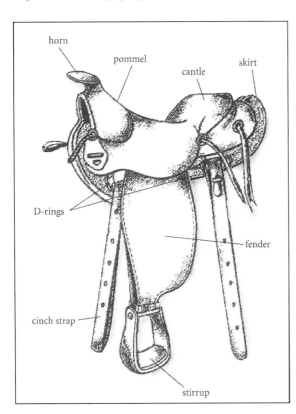

The parts of a Western saddle.

Stirrups

Western stirrups come in several shapes. A popular type is the Visalia (vis-a-LEE-a), which is shaped like a bell.

The oxbow (OKS-bo) shape has a round bottom.

Ropers use a wide type with a flat bottom so they can get off their horses easily.

The fronts of some Western stirrups are covered by tapadaros (tap-a-DARE-ohs). They are also known as taps. Taps were first used to protect the rider's feet against sharp cactus needles. Now taps help new riders keep their feet from sliding through the stirrups.

Stirrups are held on the saddle by straps called stirrup leathers. Many Western saddles have wide pieces of leather that keep the rider's legs from being rubbed by the leathers. These are called fenders.

Cinches

The cinch is a strap that keeps the saddle from falling off the horse. A Western cinch has rings at both ends. The ring attaches to straps on both sides of the saddle. These straps are called billets (BILL-its).

Some saddles use two cinches. The front cinch is usually made of cotton string. The back cinch is called the flank cinch. It is made of leather.

The flank cinch is not pulled tight. It works only when the saddle is pulled forward, such as when a cow is roped. A strap between two cinches keeps the flank cinch from hitting against the horse's belly and bothering him.

Riggings

Cinches can be attached to a Western saddle in several ways. The way the cinch is attached is called the rigging.

A center-rigged cinch is right under the middle of the saddle's seat. Forward-rigged means the cinch is in front of the middle.

Full-forward means the cinch is under the pommel. Full-forward rigging usually has a second cinch at the back of the saddle.

TYPES OF WESTERN SADDLES

The kind of Western saddle most people use has a small horn and a thick and comfortable deep seat. It weighs about thirty to thirty-five pounds.

The saddle used for calf roping is heavier and stronger, with a high horn that can hold turns of the rope. Rope turns around a horn are called dally turns.

Saddles used on cutting horses have a flat seat that helps the rider feel how the horse is moving.

Barrel-racing saddles are light, so the horse has less weight to carry.

HOW TO CHOOSE A WESTERN SADDLE

Like people, horses come in all shapes and sizes. There's no one saddle that fits every horse.

A saddle should rest comfortably over the horse's withers and back. If it's too narrow or tight, it will pinch. If it's too wide, it will slip and then fall off.

A saddle should fit you too. You belong in the middle of the seat, with your legs right under you. If the seat is too small for you, your body will be pushed forward and your legs will swing back. A seat that's too big pushes your body backward and your feet forward.

It takes lots of experience with saddles to tell whether one fits both your horse and you. That's why your friend or someone who works at a tack shop can help you find the right saddle.

Many tack shops will let you take a new saddle home to try. If you do take one home, be careful not to scratch the leather.

SADDLE BLANKETS

The most popular Western saddle blankets are made of wool and have Native American patterns. The blanket is folded in half and placed across the horse's back, under the saddle. That way, it soaks up sweat and makes the saddle sit comfortably on the horse.

When you put a saddle blanket on your horse, you must make sure there are no wrinkles or creases. Otherwise, it will rub and give your horse a sore.

ENGLISH TACK

SADDLES

The English saddle came about because of a style of jumping. Until about one hundred years ago, riders leaned back when they jumped fences. But then someone discovered that leaning forward kept riders in better balance with their horse. That made jumping easier for the horse and safer for the rider. This jumping style was called the forward seat.

The forward-seat style of jumping required a saddle with a low front, a flat seat, and pads to press your knees against. These pads are called knee rolls. This is the style many English saddles have today.

Saddles that are not used in jumping, such as for pleasure riding or for a kind of training called dressage (dre-SAHJ), have no knee rolls.

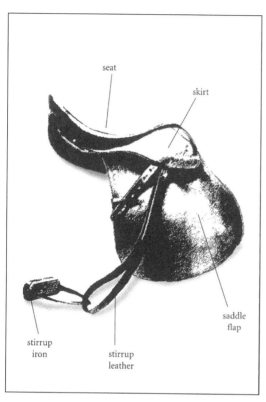

The parts of an English saddle.

Girths

Girth is the English-riding word for cinch. The girth buckles to the straps on both sides of the saddle called billets.

There are three billets, but just the two on the outside are used. The one in the middle is a spare.

Soft wool girth covers keep the girth from rubbing against the skin on a horse's stomach.

Stirrups

English stirrups are made of steel and have thin sides. Pieces of rubber on the bottom help keep your feet from slipping.

Many new riders use the release, or safety, stirrup. Instead of two steel sides, the side that's next to the rider's little toe has a strong rubber band. In case the rider falls, the rubber band lets go so that the rider's foot can easily slip out of the stirrup.

Stirrup Leathers

Like on Western saddles, stirrups are held onto English saddles by straps called leathers. They slide under the stirrup bars, then buckle together like a belt. Some leathers have numbers on their holes. That helps riders keep both stirrups even.

Here's an important safety tip: If you ride at the same hole and never change the length, the buckle will start to cut into the leather. Then the leather will wear through and break. Make sure this doesn't happen by checking the leather.

Another safety feature is the hinge on the stirrup bar. If a rider falls, the hinge swings open and the stirrup leather slides out so that the horse doesn't drag the rider along the ground.

SADDLE PAD

English-style saddle pads are made of cotton or fluffy sheepskin. Straps that slide on the saddle's billet straps keep the pad from slipping.

Some riders use a thick rubber bounce pad to protect their horse's back from the weight of the rider. The pad slides in between the saddle and the saddle pad.

HOW TO CHOOSE AN ENGLISH SADDLE

Just as with Western saddles, fitting an English saddle to both you and your horse is very important. For example, a horse with high withers needs a saddle with a high pommel.

You'll need a saddle with a seat that fits you. Otherwise, you'll slide all over your horse. Your lower legs must reach below the flaps.

When you try a saddle, ask your friend or someone at the tack shop to check how it fits both you and your horse.

Sometimes a person who buys a horse gets a saddle from the former owner. Make sure it fits you. And make sure it's in good condition. The leather, the stitching, and the hinges of the stirrup bars must all be in good shape. Otherwise, an accident might happen.

BITS AND BRIDLES

There's a big difference between Western and English saddles, but there's not a big difference between the bits that Western and English horses wear. What a horse wears depends on what he's doing and which type of bit works best for him.

As someone who's worn a bridle and a bit since I was a young horse, let me explain how they work.

BITS

A bit presses on certain parts of the horse's mouth. One place is the bars of the mouth. The bars are the spaces between the front and the back teeth.

Another place is the roof of the mouth. A bit can also press against a horse's lips or against his tongue.

Some bits work by pulling down on the crown-piece. That's the part of the bridle that runs up behind the horse's ears to his poll.

A horse has been trained to react to pressure in his mouth or on his poll. Depending on where the pressure is, he will either turn or stop.

There are two kinds of bits. One is the snaffle (SNAFF-ul). The other is the curb.

Most bits are made of a kind of steel that won't rust.

Snaffle Bits

You can tell a snaffle bit by its straight mouthpiece. Some snaffles have a mouthpiece that's in one piece. Others have two short pieces that meet in the middle. Even though these pieces can bend, people still say the mouthpiece is straight.

Snaffle bits press on the bars of the horse's mouth and on his cheeks.

The rings on the sides of the bit are for the reins.

Some snaffles have arms on their sides. These arms are called cheek-pieces. The cheek-pieces keep the rings from sliding into the horse's mouth.

Curb Bits

A curb bit has a raised mouthpiece. That's called the port. The port is often shaped like an upside-down letter U.

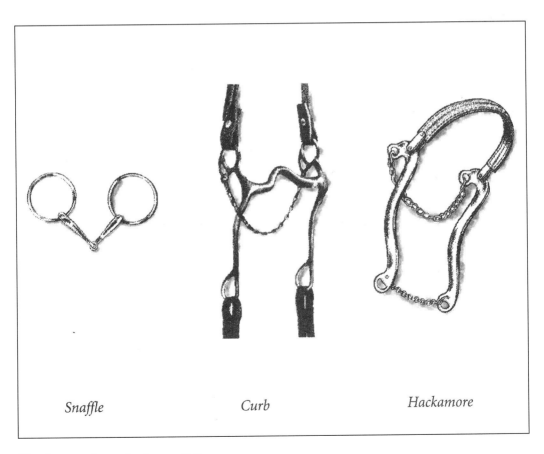

Snaffle   Curb   Hackamore

The three most popular types of bits.

Curb bits also have long arms called shanks. The reins are tied to the ends of the shanks.

When you pull on the reins, the shanks pull the bridle down against the top of the horse's head. They also make the port press against the inside of the horse's mouth. The horse is trained to stop when he feels that happen.

A grazing bit has curved shanks. They let a horse get his head close to the ground so he can eat grass.

Many curb bits have a leather strap or a metal chain. The strap or chain goes behind the horse's chin. It keeps the port from moving too far forward in the horse's mouth.

HACKAMORES

When is a bit not a bit? When it's a hackamore (HACK-a-more). That's a piece of metal that's wrapped in leather. It goes on a horse's face above his nose. When you pull on the reins, the hackamore puts pressure on the nose. The horse will then stop.

Hackamores are usually used on horses that know how to neck-rein. These horses don't need a bit to signal them to stop or turn.

CHOOSING A BIT

There are many kinds of snaffles and many kinds of curbs. The one to use depends on how well trained a horse and his rider are.

Nine times out of ten, the bit that your horse's last owner used will work just fine for you too. But in case you and your expert friend think a change of bit might make your horse go better, your friend will suggest another type.

The bit must fit your horse's mouth. A bit that's too wide will hang out of his mouth. One that's too narrow will pinch his jaw. Neither way will be comfortable for the horse. Just as important, the bit will not work very well.

BRIDLES

The job of the bridle is to hold the bit in the horse's mouth.

There are two main parts of a bridle. One is the part that goes over the horse's head. That's called the headstall. On an English bridle, it's called the crown-piece.

The other main part of an English bridle is the cheek-pieces. They hold the bit.

A buckle on the bridle lets you raise or lower the bit in the horse's mouth so it fits right. The bit is at the right height when it makes one or two wrinkles in the corners of the horse's mouth. Too many wrinkles make the horse look as if he's smiling. It also means the bit is too high. No wrinkles at all means the bit is down too low.

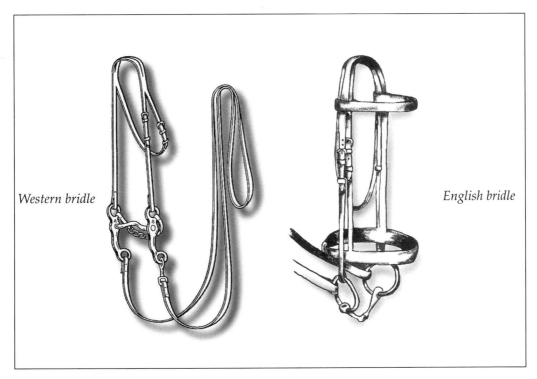

Western bridle

English bridle

Western and English bridles.

A headstall and cheek-pieces won't always keep the bridle in place. Most Western bridles have an earpiece that goes over the horse's right ear. That keeps the bridle from slipping off.

English bridles have a band that goes across the horse's head above his eyes. It's called the brow-band. Another strap called the throat latch goes behind the horse's head. Both the brow-band and throat latch help keep the bridle from slipping off.

REINS

Reins for Western bridles come in two styles. Split reins are two long leather straps. They're never tied together. You usually carry both of them in one of your hands.

The other style is one long rein with a ring at the end. A four-foot strap called the romal (ro-MAL) is tied or snapped to the ring. You hold the romal with one hand just behind the ring. With your other hand, you hold the rest of the romal farther back.

Reins for an English bridle are two straps buckled together to make a single loop that goes from one side of the bit to its other side. These reins are usually held with both hands.

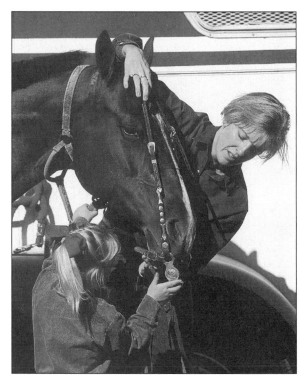

Keeping a halter around a horse's neck until the bridle is in place prevents the animal from wandering off. (AQHA photo by Wyatt McSpadden)

OTHER TACK

MARTINGALES AND TIE-DOWNS

A horse that lifts or tosses his head can be a real problem—especially when he lifts his head really high just when you lean forward. Ker-bump goes your nose against his neck!

A cure for this problem is a leather strap that runs between the horse's front legs from the cinch or girth to a noseband around the horse's face. The strap is called a martingale (MAR-tin-gale). Westerners call it a tie-down. The martingale is kept just tight enough to keep the horse from lifting his head too far.

Some horses like to stop and graze during a trail ride when their riders don't want them to. A side-check keeps that from happening. That's a strap or rope that goes from the pommel of the saddle to the top of the bridle's cheek-piece. Many new riders have been kept from being pulled over their horse's head by a side-check.

BREAST-COLLAR

A breast-collar keeps the saddle from slipping. A leather strap goes across the horse's chest. Another strap goes over the withers. Together they hold the saddle in place.

Horses used for roping or other events often wear a breast-collar.

This horse is wearing a breast-collar.

HALTERS

Can you guess which piece of tack a horse wears more than any other?

That's right—it's his halter.

Halters have many uses. You'll use a halter to lead your horse when he's not wearing a bridle. The halter also makes a horse easier to catch when he's out in a pasture. You can use a halter to tie your horse to a fence or in his stall and he won't wander away.

Halters are made of rope, webbing, or leather. Leather halters are used for more important times such as horse-show halter and showmanship classes.

You know a halter fits right when you can easily slide two of your fingers under the halter at the horse's cheeks and behind his jaw. A halter that's too tight makes it hard for the horse to breathe.

A horse that's wearing a halter can be held or led easily and safely. (AQHA photo by Wyatt McSpadden)

We've all seen cowboy movies where riders tie their reins to a hitching rail. That works only in the movies. Tying a horse by his reins is very dangerous. If the horse pulls back, the bit will hurt his mouth. That's why you always tie a horse by using a halter. The horse can wear the halter by itself, or it can go over his bridle if he's wearing a bridle when you want to tie him.

CLEANING TACK

Sweat and dirt are bad for leather, so tack should be cleaned after every time you use it.

A special soap called saddle soap is used for cleaning. Work a little bit of saddle soap into the leather with a damp sponge. Don't use too much, or the leather will become sticky. Rinse the sponge often to get rid of any dirt that comes off the saddle or bridle.

Your tack will need a very good cleaning once in a while. How often you'll need to do this job depends on how dirty the tack gets. Your friend can tell you about that.

Cleaning your tack after every ride keeps the leather clean and soft. (AQHA photo by Wyatt McSpadden)

Start by taking the saddle and bridle apart. Bits, stirrup irons, and other pieces of metal should go into a bowl or bucket of clean water. Saddle pads and saddle blankets can be cleaned in a washing machine.

Clean each piece of leather with saddle soap on a damp sponge. Any piece that is very dry or dirty needs help from a special cleaner called leather dressing. Dressing puts oil back into the leather. The oil keeps the leather soft. Don't use too much or the leather will become too soft and sticky.

Then clean the metal pieces with metal polish. Wipe away all the polish from the metal, especially from the bit. Then dip the metal in clean water and dry the pieces.

Before you put the saddle or bridle back together, rub the leather with a soft clean towel to give it a nice shine.

Wet tack that's been out in the rain or snow needs to be dried. Sunlight or heat from a radiator makes leather dry out too fast. Then the leather will crack. Let the leather dry out on its own. Then use saddle soap or leather dressing to put the oil back in.

Just the way that grooming a horse is a good time to look for cuts, scrapes, and loose shoes, cleaning tack lets you look for problems. If you see any leather that's worn out or stitches that are torn, show the saddle or bridle to your friend or your riding instructor.

Most tack shops can fix tack that's worn or torn. However, if any part of a saddle or bridle can't be fixed as good as new, you'll have to get another one.

Storing Tack

Putting a saddle flat on the ground hurts its tree. Instead, stand the saddle up against a wall or fence whenever it's not on a horse. Inside your barn, it belongs on a saddle rack in the tack room.

Hanging a bridle, martingale, or breast-collar on a thin nail stretches the leather. A bridle rack is better.

A cloth bag or case keeps leather from being scratched. Keeping tack in a case is a good idea when you go somewhere, like to a horse show.

Even if you use a bag or case, make sure your saddle can't bounce around in the back of your truck or trailer. That way, if the truck hits a bump, the saddle won't go flying and land flat on its tree.

BLANKETS

Horses that live where winters are cold will want to wear a blanket, especially at night. Blankets come in different styles. Some are quilted, like ski jackets. Others are made of wool.

Even if you live where it never gets very cold, a light blanket called a cooler keeps a horse from catching a chill after being ridden or given a bath.

Straps and buckles on blankets and coolers keep them in place.

Horse clothing comes in different styles and sizes, just like clothing for people. Your friend or someone at a tack store can help you pick what's best for your horse.

FOR FURTHER INFORMATION:

People who compete in AQHA horse shows must know the rules about the right kind of tack for the events they want to take part in. You can learn the rules by reading AQHA's *Official Handbook of Rules & Regulations*.

8

FEEDING YOUR AMERICAN QUARTER HORSE

Did I hear you say it's dinnertime?

I hope so, because I love to eat. All horses do. And what we eat is very important.

GRASS

Horses that lived outdoors many years ago never had to work hard to find food. Food was always as close as the grass at their feet.

Even now, horses that live in pastures spend lots of time eating grass. That's called grazing.

Grazing is a way to get good, healthy food. Just as important, grazing keeps a horse busy. Most horses hate to be bored, so grazing keeps us very happy.

Hay

Hay is made of long pieces of grass that have been dried out.

All horses, even those that live in pastures, need to eat hay. Hay helps other food move through the horse's body.

A popular type is called alfalfa (al-FAL-fa). Other types are clover, timothy (TIM-o-thee), and redtop. In some parts of the country, redtop is called redtip.

Sometimes horses are fed only one kind of hay. However, they often eat two or more types that are mixed together.

Your friend or the vet will tell you what kind of hay to feed your horse.

Whatever type of hay you feed your horse, it must be good. Good hay is green in color (brown hay isn't very good). Good hay smells sweet, and it doesn't have any dust or dirt in it.

After hay is dried, it's put into big heavy blocks. Each block is called a bale. Blocks of hay are easier to carry and store than loose hay.

A bale easily comes apart into slices. Each slice is called a flake and is about as wide as a grown-up person's hand.

A horse is usually fed a few flakes of hay in the morning and a few more in the afternoon or evening.

Hay comes in other forms. It can be pressed together into cubes. Bags of hay cubes are easy to store and to feed, but they cost more than hay that comes in bales.

Grain and Feed

Horses that aren't ridden can eat nothing but grass. That's because they don't do any work. But horses that are ridden need the kind of food that makes them strong. That food is grain. It's the same kind of grain that goes into breakfast cereals and into bread.

One kind of grain is oats. Oats give a horse lots of strength, and they're easy to eat too.

Other grains are corn and bran, which is the outside of wheat or of oats.

Although crushed beets aren't really a grain, they can help a thin horse put on weight. The crushed beets must be soaked in water for at least eight to ten hours before a horse can eat them.

Other kinds of grain are made into something called feed. They come in big bags, like dry dog or cat food.

Sweet feed has a kind of sugar that horses love. Another kind of feed is made of food that has been squeezed together into tiny pieces called pellets.

Horse owners who don't have much space to store food like to use sweet feed or pellets.

What to feed your horse depends on how old he is and how much work he does. A horse that gets too much to eat can become too strong and too hard to ride. He can also become too fat.

Like with hay, your friend or the vet can tell you what and how much to feed.

Most horses are fed twice a day, once in the morning and again in the late afternoon. Once you've started your horse on that schedule, please stick to it. Remember that horses like everything done the same way all the time. They become upset when their meals are late, especially when they're in their stalls.

However, if you and your horse go out for a long trail ride in the afternoon and you usually feed him at 3:00, you don't have to take feed along. You can wait till you get home and your horse is all cooled off. Then you can feed him.

Your horse should get his grain or pellets in the feed bin in his stall. If he's out in his pasture, put the feed in a bucket or tub. The bucket or tub should have a flat bottom. Otherwise, the horse will knock it over and spill all his feed.

Some people put hay on the floor of the stall. Other people put the hay in a net. The hay net should be hung high enough so the horse can't lift his leg and put his foot in it.

Flakes of hay can be put on the ground in a pasture. Place them on a dry, clean piece of ground or on grass.

Dry hay makes some horses cough and sneeze. They need hay that has been soaked in water. If your friend tells you to, soak the hay until it's *really* wet.

Just as you shouldn't jump into the swimming pool right after you eat, horses need to rest after they eat so that they don't get a

bellyache. Wait at least a half hour after your horse finishes eating before you ride him.

And never let a horse eat or drink while he's still hot after being ridden. He needs to cool off before getting his dinner.

SALT

Horses know that salt is good for them, and they like to lick a block of salt. Every stall and pasture should have a salt block.

WATER

Horses need water as much as they need solid food.

A grown-up horse needs to drink at least eight to ten gallons of water every day. That's between 130 and 150 glasses of water! And they need even more water on a hot day or when they've done lots of work.

A horse must be able to have water to drink all the time. It can come from a stream or a pond in a pasture. Or a tub or buckets in the pasture or buckets in a stall.

Horses are fussy about what they drink. They don't like water that's dirty or has things floating around in it. That's why you've

got to keep water buckets and tubs clean.

TREATS

Horses love treats and snacks as much as people do. A few carrots or an apple make excellent treats. So do lumps of sugar, although not every horse likes sugar.

Many people break carrots in half and cut apples into small pieces. That makes them easier to eat.

A horse's teeth can't always tell the difference between a piece of carrot and the fingers that are holding it. Be sure to hold your hand flat and keep your fingers out of the way.

Some horses will start thinking there's a treat waiting whenever they see a person's hand. They start nipping at any hand they see. That's why some people never give treats by hand. They put them in the horse's feed bin. That's safer, and those horses love their people just as much.

9

GROOMING YOUR AMERICAN QUARTER HORSE

Hello, it's Two Bits here. Keeping your horse neat and clean is just as important as keeping yourself neat and clean. And it's lots more fun.

Cleaning a horse is called grooming. Grooming gets rid of dirt and dried sweat. If the dirt and sweat stay on the horse, he might get sores on his skin.

Grooming also makes the horse look and feel good. You'll be proud to hear people say that you take good care of him.

Will you be able to brush your horse, or clean his feet, or give him a bath? That all depends on how tall and how strong you are. You won't want to do anything that isn't safe for you and the horse. That's something to talk about with your friend and your folks.

Even if you can't do very much grooming by yourself, you still should know how to do it. And you can help the person who grooms your horse.

Grooming is a good time to see whether your horse has any cuts or sores or anything else that needs fixing. You can certainly help look.

Besides, your horse likes it when you're with him.

Your horse will need to be groomed before each time you ride him. Take special care to clean his back. Dirt that gets under the saddle can cause sores.

You'll need the right tools:

- a metal or rubber comb called a curry comb. The curry comb scrapes away mud and dried dirt.
- a hard hairbrush. This brush wipes away the dirt that the curry comb loosens.
- a soft brush to take off smaller pieces of dirt and loose hair.
- a mane comb. This small metal comb is used to clean the horse's mane.
- a long thin metal tool called a sweat scraper. The sweat scraper wipes away water after a bath.
- a sponge to clean the horse's face.
- a small metal tool called a hoof pick. The hoof pick cleans away dirt and rocks from the bottom of the horse's feet.

If you don't tie your horse to a fence, a barn wall, or a tree while you groom him, he'll walk away.

Use a rope that snaps onto his halter. Take care that the rope is no lower than the horse's head. That's to make sure he won't be able to step over the rope.

Cross tying a horse in the aisle of a barn keeps him from walking away while you're grooming or tacking him. (The Quarter Horse Journal)

Two ropes keep a horse from moving better than one rope does. This is called cross tying. One rope goes on one side of the halter and the other rope goes on the other side. The other ends of both ropes are tied to the walls along the barn's aisle.

BRUSHING

Brush a horse from his top to his toes. That way, the dirt will easily fall off. You won't have to go back and clean places that you already cleaned.

Start with the curry comb. Brush his neck, body, and the tops of his legs. Rub in small circles to loosen any mud and dried sweat. The curry comb is hard, so don't brush the horse's face or below his knees and hocks.

Clean dirt out of the curry comb by banging it against the ground or the barn wall.

Then use the hard brush to get rid of dirt that's still on the horse. Brush all over the horse's body and all the way down to his feet. Brush his tail too.

The mane comb is used only on the mane. It shouldn't be used on the tail because the teeth will break the tail hairs. Comb small pieces of mane at a time. Use your fingers to pull out anything you can't comb away.

Clean your horse's face with the soft brush. Brush gently with one hand. Use your other hand to keep dust out of his eyes.

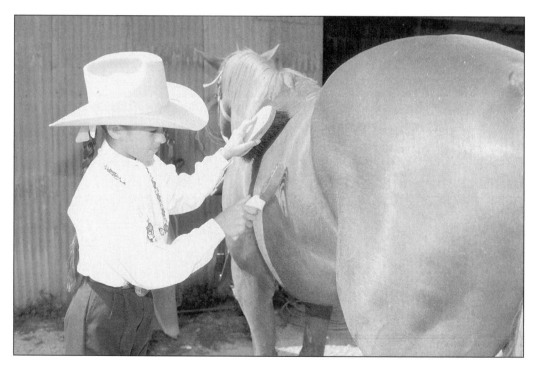

First loosen the dirt with a metal curry comb. Then brush it off with a body brush. (AQHA photo by Wyatt McSpadden)

Be careful of your horse's eyes when you brush his forelock. (AQHA photo by Wyatt McSpadden)

Then wipe around his eyes and nose with a sponge. The sponge should be damp, not soaking wet.

You don't need to groom your horse this well after you ride him. But you'll still need to brush or sponge away any sweat stains. Wait until the horse is cool before you clean him after a ride.

CLEANING HOOVES

Dirt, bedding, little rocks, and other things can get caught in the bottom of a horse's foot. That's why you've got to scrape the bottom clean before and after you ride.

Lifting and holding a horse's foot is not easy for anyone, especially for a young person. But you should know how to clean out feet so that you'll be able to do it when you're older. Watch your friend clean them, and if your friend thinks you're big enough, you can try while your friend watches.

To lift a horse's left front foot, stand close to his left side. Face his tail and reach around the left front leg with your left hand. Slide your hand down the back of the leg. Stop when you get to the fetlock, then lift the foot. Say the word "lift" or "up."

If the horse doesn't lift his foot right away, give the leg a little pinch with your thumb and first finger. At the same time, lean your body against the horse's body.

Once the foot is off the ground, hold it up with your left hand. This may not be easy to do. Horses that don't mind lifting a foot sometimes don't like to keep the foot in the air for more than a few seconds. But if your friend thinks it's safe, keep holding the foot.

Holding the hoof pick in your right hand, scrape the bottom of the foot. Keep the tip of the pick pointed away from you. That way, you won't poke yourself if the pick slips.

Scrape from the back of the foot toward the front. Scrape between the frog and the outside part of the foot. Use the pick just hard enough to clean out any dirt and rocks. Be careful not to scratch the frog with the hoof pick.

Then clean the other feet. Lift and hold the feet on the horse's left side with your left hand. Use your right hand to lift and hold the feet on his right side.

Cleaning your horse's feet is a good time to make sure his shoes are on tight. If you see a shoe that's loose or one that's missing a nail, tell your friend. Then a farrier can come to fix the shoe.

Keeping your horse on cross-ties when you're finished grooming him isn't very fair. A fly may be buzzing around and he can't reach it. Or he may have a bad itch that he can't scratch. Put your horse back in his stall, even if it's only a little while till you'll ride him again.

BATHS

Nothing is more fun on a warm day than giving your horse a bath. It's even better when you can cool yourself off too!

You can use water from a bucket or from a hose. Using a hose may make it easier to get water all over the horse's body.

Use warm water, never cold water. Wash the horse from his neck back to his tail and from the top of his back to the ground. Don't spray any water in his face or in his ears.

Horses love a bath on a hot day. Remember to keep the hose water out of his face. (AQHA photo by Wyatt McSpadden)

Water will stay in the hair on the horse's body. To get it off, use the sweat scraper. Use its edge and scrape just hard enough to get the water off. When you get to the legs, don't scrape any lower than the knees and hocks.

A wet horse that stands around can catch a chill, even on a warm day. That's why you have to walk the horse around until he's as dry as can be.

There's another reason. If you put a wet horse out in his pasture, he'll lie down and roll around. Then he'll be even dirtier than before you gave him his bath!

At least once a week during warm weather, you'll want to give your horse a bath with soap. There's special soap for cleaning horses that your friend can help you find.

If you use soap too often, it will take all the oil out of his hair and skin. That kind of oil keeps the horse's hair and skin healthy.

Here's what to do:

After you clean the horse with plain water, fill a bucket with warm water and add a little soap.

Use a sponge and start at the top of the horse's body. Doing a small area at a time, rub the soap into the horse's coat. Wash one side of the horse all the way down to the feet. Then do the other side.

Be especially careful not to get any soap in the horse's eyes or ears. Only clean water without soap belongs on the horse's face.

When you do the mane and tail, soak the long hairs as well as you can.

When you're finished, wash away all the soap with clean warm water.

After you use the sweat scraper to get the water off the horse, walk him around until he's dry.

Here are some other grooming jobs that you should know about.

PULLING MANES AND TAILS

Several times a year your horse's mane and tail may need to be made thinner and shorter. That's how horses get haircuts.

A horse's hair doesn't all grow at the same speed. That's why you'll see your friend comb a small bunch of mane hair and then pull out some of the longest hairs. That will make the mane even and thinner.

This job is called pulling. Don't worry—pulling doesn't hurt the horse at all.

Your friend will also pull out some of the longer hairs of your horse's tail. That doesn't hurt either.

Some owners trim or cut the hair on the mane. That gives the horse a kind of crew cut!

CLIPPING

Clipping gives a horse a haircut on his body. Your friend will probably use electric clippers. Most horses don't mind the sound the clippers make.

How often a horse needs to be clipped depends on how fast and how thick his hair grows.

Clipping a horse keeps him cooler in hot weather. It also lets sweat dry faster.

How many of these jobs you can do by yourself depends on your age and your size. But remember, no matter who else grooms your horse, there's always something you can do to help.

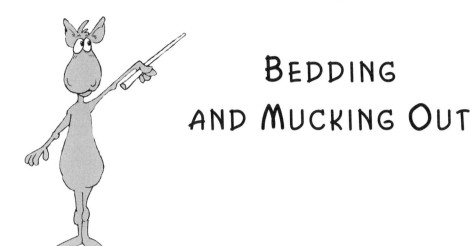

10

BEDDING
AND MUCKING OUT

How would you like to stand on a hard floor all day? Or sleep in a bed that has no mattress? Well, neither would your horse.

That's why your horse's stall should have something on its floor called bedding. Bedding is like a mattress or a carpet. It's comfortable to stand on or lie down on. Bedding also soaks up the wetness after your horse goes to the bathroom in his stall.

Many years ago, all horse owners used straw as bedding. Straw is dried grass, like hay, but it's not good to eat.

These days, most people use wood shavings or sawdust. Shavings are very thin pieces of wood. Sawdust is a kind of powder made of wood. You can buy shavings and sawdust in very large bags.

Many people like shavings better than sawdust because sawdust gets into hard clumps when it's wet.

Some people still use straw. Straw soaks up wetness very well, but some horses try to eat it. Since straw isn't good for a horse, only those horses that don't like to eat straw should have it in their stall.

Bedding must cover the whole stall about six inches deep. Some horses like to sleep standing up. If yours likes to sleep lying down, you can make the bedding a little deeper. That would make a more comfortable mattress for him.

MUCKING OUT

Cleaning a stall is called mucking out. Although it's not the most fun part of owning a horse, mucking out isn't too bad a job once you get used to it.

How often you'll have to muck out your horse's stall depends on how much time he spends in it. If he's inside only at night, you'll have to clean it once a day. That would be in the morning, after your horse finishes his breakfast.

On days when your horse is in his stall for a long time, you'll want to pick up manure whenever you see it. That way, he'll have a cleaner stall and you won't have a lot to carry out at the end of the day.

Tools for mucking out are a special manure fork, a regular pitchfork, a broom, a shovel, and a wheelbarrow.

Of course, you can't clean the stall while your horse is in there. You'll have to move him outside the stall or put him out in his pasture.

Start cleaning by picking up the largest pieces of manure with the manure fork. Put them in the wheelbarrow.

The smaller pieces, especially any that the horse has stepped on, may have to be dug out of the bedding. Take only the manure. Leave as much of the dry bedding as you can. If you've ever cleaned a cat's litter box, you'll know what to do.

Some bedding will be damp. Spread that around the stall. It will dry out that way.

Some bedding will be very wet. That goes into the wheelbarrow.

Take the manure and dirty bedding to the manure pile. Be careful, though. A full wheelbarrow is very heavy. Don't hurt yourself trying to lift one. Instead, fill the wheelbarrow only with as much as you can push. You may have to make several trips.

Then use the broom and shovel to sweep any bedding on the barn floor back into the stall.

Bedding that becomes very wet and dirty will have to be changed. How often to do it depends on how much time your horse spends in his stall. Your friend will tell you.

When it's time to change the bedding, first muck out the stall the way you do every day. But this time, also take all the wet bedding out to the manure pile.

Then push all the dry bedding to one side of the stall. Use the pitchfork or broom.

Let the stall air out as long as your horse can stay outdoors. If your horse can stay outside all day, that's great. The longer, the better.

Before your horse is ready to come inside, push the dry bedding back as a bottom layer. Then add fresh bedding.

Your horse will like his stall as much as you like having clean sheets on your bed!

Manure in the riding ring should be taken to the manure pile.

Sometimes manure in your horse's pasture should go to the manure pile. However, some of it can sometimes be spread around the pasture. When it dries out, it will help make the grass grow.

You won't want to let the manure pile get too big. Sometimes a farmer will be happy to come and get it. Other times, your folks will have to take it to a place where people are allowed to dump manure.

The best way to learn about mucking out is by doing it yourself. Anyone who has a horse will be more than happy to show you how and then watch you do it.

11

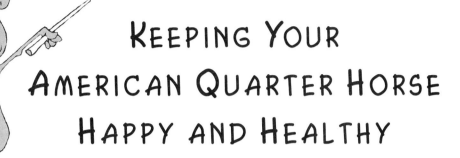

KEEPING YOUR AMERICAN QUARTER HORSE HAPPY AND HEALTHY

Hi, it's Doctor Two Bits with a question for you. How can you tell when a horse isn't feeling well?

The answer is, he'll tell you.

No, he won't say, "Oh, dear me, I don't feel well." But he'll tell you the way horses tell people things: by how they look and act.

Your folks don't call a doctor every time you're sick or every time you hurt yourself. They know lots of ways to make you feel

RUSH 96

better. But when something serious happens, they'll call a doctor.

The same thing will happen with your horse. Most of the time, your friend or another grown-up will make your horse feel better. Sometimes you can too, at least after you learn how. But other times a veterinarian—remember, that's a horse doctor—will have to come.

The vet may ask you to hold your horse while he or she examines him. You may also be asked to walk or jog the horse around. Whatever you do is important, because it makes you part of the team of people who care for your horse.

PREPARING FOR ACCIDENTS

Every barn needs special supplies in case an accident happens. Some of them are:

- scissors
- hair clippers
- special soap and powder for putting on cuts
- bandages and pads for cuts
- a big roll of cotton
- clean towels

Your vet will suggest many other supplies.

Whenever you take the scissors or the tape or anything else out of the supplies box, you should put it back as soon as you finish using it. Then, people will be able to find it quickly when an accident happens.

CUTS

Just like people, horses sometimes fall or bump into something sharp. They cut themselves.

If you see that your horse is bleeding, call a grown-up in a hurry. The grown-up will decide how bad the cut is.

Sometimes the grown-up can stop the bleeding, but other times the vet will have to come.

HEATSTROKE

Being out in the sun on a very hot summer day can sometimes make the horse sick. That's called heatstroke.

A horse that is getting heatstroke will stop sweating. He will have trouble breathing, and he won't feel like moving.

The very first thing to do is get the horse out of the sun. Move him under a tree or in the shade of a barn or a house. Then run and call a grown-up.

You and the grown-up should put cool water over the horse's head. Use a hose or a sponge. Don't use cold water, and do not let the horse drink anything.

If you ride on a very hot day, ride early in the morning or late in the afternoon. Try not to go out at noon, when the sun is at its hottest.

Both you and your horse will enjoy the ride much more.

COLIC

Horses can get stomach-aches. A stomach-ache for horses is called colic.

Horses can get colic in different ways; for example, if they eat too much or eat the wrong kind of food. They can get colic from drinking water that's too cold, especially when they're hot and sweaty after being ridden. They can get colic when food gets stuck in their stomach.

We all know how much bellyaches can hurt. Horses try to get rid of the pain by biting at their sides. They walk around in circles. They lie down and roll on their back.

Sometimes, though, they just stand very still. They sweat and they look unhappy.

If you see your horse doing any of these things, run and call a grown-up. The grown-up will then call the vet.

Until the vet comes, it's very important to keep the horse on his feet. Walk him around slowly, and don't let him lie down.

The vet will then give the horse medicine to make him feel better.

SORE FEET AND LEGS

One day you may take your horse out of his pasture or his stall and see that he's limping. Or while you're riding, your horse takes a funny step and then acts as though his foot or his leg is hurting him.

Although American Quarter Horses have strong legs and feet, any horse can become lame. Lame is the word that means having trouble moving.

As soon as you think something doesn't look or feel right about the way your horse is moving, you should tell your friend.

In most cases your friend can help the horse without having to call a vet. The problem may be just a little piece of rock that's stuck in the horse's foot. Maybe he twisted an ankle.

Then the horse will need to rest for one or two days, but perhaps even longer. Of course, you won't be able to ride him until he's all better.

Some problems can be serious enough for the vet to have to come. The vet will give your horse medicine to make him feel better. The horse will then have to rest for a while. The vet will tell you how long that will be.

THRUSH

Thrush is a disease of the frog, the soft part on the bottom of a horse's foot. It's easy to tell when a horse has thrush: The black stuff that comes out of the frog has one of the worst smells in the world.

The vet will clean out the bad part of the frog. Then the vet will put medicine on the foot.

Horses that live in a clean, dry stall or pasture seldom get thrush.

Cough

Just like with humans, a horse that coughs once in a while isn't sick. But lots of coughing is bad.

The vet will give the horse a kind of cough medicine. Then the horse will have to rest until the cough goes away.

That sounds just like when you get a cough, doesn't it?

Hay that's full of dust can make a horse cough. That's why you always want to give your horse the best hay you can find.

Worms and Insects

Very tiny worms and insects live in pastures. They get into a horse's body when he eats the grass they're in.

Once inside the horse, they can make him sick. However, he won't get sick if he's given a special medicine. Sometimes it comes in a tube like toothpaste does.

Your friend or the vet will give your horse this medicine every few months. This job is called worming.

These worms and insects don't like to live in clean pastures. That's why clearing pastures of manure helps keep your horse healthy.

Teeth

A horse's teeth keep growing as long as he lives. Eating grain helps keep the teeth smooth, but sometimes they grow sharp edges that cut the inside of his mouth.

A vet will smooth the edges down with a tool called a rasp. A rasp looks like a very big nail file.

The job of smoothing the edges is called floating the teeth. And no, it doesn't hurt the horse at all.

One way to tell that your horse's teeth may be hurting him is when he doesn't want you to put the bit in his mouth. Or he may toss his head up and down when he's wearing his bridle. That's how he tries to get away from the pain.

If you think your horse is trying to tell you that his teeth hurt, tell your friend. Do *not* try to look in his mouth yourself. Horse teeth are very sharp, and even though he doesn't mean to bite you, he might by accident.

One last thought from Doctor Two Bits: Because a horse tells you he doesn't feel well by the way he looks and acts, it's up to you to learn what he looks and acts like when he's healthy.

That's how you'll be able to tell the difference.

FOR FURTHER INFORMATION:

AQHA has a video called *Your Horse's Health*. A vet talks about how to keep your horse healthy. 19 minutes.

A group of vets called the American Association of Equine Practitioners has a video called *A Veterinarian . . . For the Life of Your Horse*. It's about how vets examine horses. AQHA will lend you the video, or you can buy a copy by calling the American Association of Equine Practitioners at 1-800-GET-ADVM.

12

LET'S GO
TO A HORSE SHOW

Riding a horse is fun, and so is watching other people ride. It's even more fun to watch them when they're riding in a horse show. That's an event where the best horses and riders win prizes.

You can find horse shows all over the country. Lots of stables put on their own shows for the people who ride there. Maybe the place where you ride holds one.

Some horse shows are small, with fewer than one hundred or fifty horses and riders. Big shows may have thousands of horses. Small shows take only one day. Big ones last for two weeks or even longer.

We'll want to see all the things American Quarter Horses do at horse shows, so we'll have to make believe we're going to a very big one.

Okay, here we are. We're at a big horse show, with thousands of other people who have come to watch. We're in our seats. But while we wait for the show to start, let's learn a few words that will help us understand how a horse show works.

The big ring where horse-show events are held is often called an arena. Some arenas are outdoors, and some are indoors.

Each event is called a class. Some classes are for people who ride just for the fun of it. Those people are called amateurs (AM-a-churs). Other classes are for people who earn money working with horses. They are called professionals. Still other classes are for youth riders who, just like you, are younger than eighteen years old.

Horses and riders that do well are given prize ribbons. The ribbons come in a rainbow of colors. Each color shows how the horse or rider did in that class:

The **blue** ribbon is for first place,
red is for second place,
white is for third place,
yellow is for fourth place,
pink is for fifth place,
green is for sixth place,
purple is for seventh place,
brown is for eighth place.

A division is the word for all the classes that a horse does; for example, the halter division or the jumper division. The horse or the rider that gets the highest score in a division is known as the champion. The one that finishes in second place is known as the reserve. Both the champion and the reserve are given ribbons made up of three colors. The champion gets a ribbon of blue, red, and white. The reserve's ribbon is red, white, and yellow.

Okay, now let's find our seats, sit back, and watch the horse show.

WESTERN CLASSES

Halter and showmanship classes are very popular with American Quarter Horse owners of all ages. (AQHA photo by Wyatt McSpadden)

HALTER

The horses that take part in halter classes are judged on how much they look like what people say the perfect American Quarter Horse should look like.

The people who show the horses to the judges are called handlers. Handlers lead their horses into the arena and then line up.

The judge looks at each horse to see how well the horse is built. To see how the horse moves, the judge will ask the handler to jog the horse a short way.

Judging halter horses is not an easy job. Not only are the horses compared to what a perfect American Quarter Horse should look like, the judges compare them to the other horses in the class.

That means the judge must decide which horse has the prettiest head and the nicest legs and the best other parts of the body. Judging this way takes time, and it takes a judge who knows a lot about American Quarter Horses.

SHOWMANSHIP

Showmanship is a halter class, but here the handler, not the horse, is being judged.

The judge watches the way each handler leads his or her horse; for example, how well the handler walks the horse to one end of the arena, then turns the horse and makes him take a few steps backward. It's important that the horse stand quietly while the judge looks at him up close.

It's also important that the horse look neat and clean. That's proof that the handler groomed him as well as possible.

WESTERN PLEASURE

The name of this class says just what the judges are looking for. They want to see horses that look like a pleasure to ride.

That means the horses should have a comfortable walk, jog, and lope. It also means good manners. In fact, all the rider should have to do is sit back and enjoy the ride.

Horses are judged in a group. After they've gone around the arena both ways at the walk, jog, and lope, the judge will ask the riders to make them take a few steps backward.

That may sound easy, but any judge or rider will tell you that winning a Western pleasure class takes skill. It also takes a really nice horse.

TRAIL

If you've gone on a trail ride, you know you can find lots of interesting things along the way. There may be a gate you have to open and shut. Your horse may have to cross a bridge or walk over a pile of logs. You'd want to be on a horse that would easily do everything you asked.

That's what the judge of a trail class is looking for. The judge wants to see a calm and safe horse that isn't bothered by anything he finds on the trail.

One at a time, the horses in this class go around the arena. There may be a gate that the rider must open and close. After walking over a pile of logs, the horse may have to back up between logs on the ground in a variety of shapes, often a T. Then the horse must stand still as the rider puts on a raincoat while still on the horse's back. Or maybe the horse will walk across a little wooden bridge and then walk sideways for several steps.

The horses are scored on how well they handle each problem. They can get extra points for good manners and for showing lots of interest in what they're doing.

I bet that's just the sort of horse you'd like to ride on a trail ride.

REINING

Reining classes are always fun. That's because the horses do exciting things. They spin, they race down the arena, then they slide to a stop.

These moves are for more than just showing off. They show the kind of skills a horse needs to work cattle.

The way all the moves are put together is called a pattern.

Circles and figure eights are important parts of a pattern. The judge wants to see a round circle, not a wiggly one. It should be done at a smooth and steady lope. A figure eight is two circles that meet at the halfway point, like the number 8. These circles should also be round, not wiggly.

In the rundown, the horse lopes down the middle of the arena. Then comes the sliding stop. The horse seems to sit down on his hind end while his front legs keep moving until he comes to a complete stop. It happens so fast that the horse's feet kick up a shower of dirt! Some people in the crowd get so excited when they see a good sliding stop, they clap and cheer.

The spin happens just as fast as the sliding stop. Here the horse keeps one hind foot on the ground and turns his body in a complete circle around that foot.

Another move is the rollback. The horse stops, spins a half turn, then lopes off in the opposite direction. It's all done very fast and in one quick move.

In the sliding stop, a reining horse's hind end seems to melt into the ground. (AQHA photo by Wyatt McSpadden)

The judge scores each part of the pattern. A horse starts with a score of 70 points. Points are added or taken away depending on how well or how poorly he does each of the moves. The horse with the highest score wins the class.

WESTERN RIDING

Western riding classes use many of the same moves that reining and trail classes do. However, here the judge wants to see how well each horse listens to his rider's signals.

These classes also have a pattern that every horse does. One pattern starts with the horse entering the arena at a walk, jogging over a single log, and then loping.

Then the horse weaves around five traffic cones that are placed thirty to fifty feet apart down the long side of the arena. The horse lopes around the cones, while the judge watches to see how well the horse changes from one lead to the other as he goes from one cone to the next.

The horse then goes back up the arena and over the log. At the end of the arena, the horse turns and moves down the centerline, where he stops and backs a few steps.

Like reining classes, each move in the pattern is scored. A horse starts with a score of 70. Points are added or taken away depending on how well or how poorly the horse does. The winner is the horse with the highest score.

WORKING COW HORSE

A working cow horse class is really two classes in one. First a horse shows he has been trained to work (remember, that's another word for move) a cow. Then he actually works one.

The first part is called the dry work. Horses do a pattern like in a reining class: circles and figure eights, rundowns, rollbacks, and spins.

The second half is called the cow work. It starts with the horse and rider not letting a cow move from one end of the arena. Then they let the cow run down along the rail on the long side of the arena. The rider gets his horse in front of the cow. Then the horse turns the cow in circles—first one way, then the other way.

The cow work ends with the horse and rider moving the cow to the center of the arena. There the horse turns the cow in circles again—first one way, then the other. Turning the cow in the center of the arena is hard, because there's no fence to keep the cow from running away.

Each horse has two minutes to work a cow. They can earn scores of 60 to 80 points. Horses lose points by letting the cow get away or from needing too many signals from the rider.

In a working cow horse class, the horse and rider must turn the cow in the middle of the arena. (AQHA photo by Wyatt McSpadden)

WESTERN HORSEMANSHIP

Except in showmanship, only the horses have been judged in all the classes we've seen so far. But because how a rider sits in the saddle and controls the horse are very important, AQHA horse shows have horsemanship classes for amateur and youth riders. Horsemanship means skill at riding.

All the riders in a Western horsemanship class do a pattern that lasts for thirty seconds. The judge may ask them to ride in a straight line and make a circle at the jog and the lope. They may back up, change leads at the lope, and do a spin and a rollback. Some judges even ask riders to get off their horses and get back on again.

Riders who earn good scores go on to the second part of the class. Then they work all at once as a group. The judge will ask them to walk, jog, and lope both ways around the arena. The judge will look at how well the riders sit and how well they steer their horses. The riders will get good marks if their horses make smooth changes from one gait to another.

If the judge can't choose a winner, he will ask the riders he likes to do more work.

Western horsemanship classes are good for young riders like you to watch. Is that boy on the sorrel horse keeping his legs against his horse's sides the right way? Is that girl on the gray horse sitting while her horse jogs or is she bouncing around?

It's fun to make believe you're the judge and pick the winner of the class.

CALF ROPING

You may have seen calf roping at a rodeo. There it's judged on how fast a cowboy can rope and tie a calf. However, calf roping at AQHA horse shows is judged in a different way. It's judged on how well the horse helps his rider rope the calf.

The judging starts when the horse walks into the starting area. He should stand quietly, but be ready to move at his rider's signal.

Once the calf is turned loose, the horse should leave the starting area quickly and lope right behind the calf. It's important that the horse move on his own, because the rider is swinging his rope over his head and isn't able to steer.

As soon as the rider ropes the calf, the horse stops quickly in the same sliding stop we saw in the reining class. The rider wraps the end of the rope around the saddle horn (that's called dallying), then gets off and runs toward the calf. The horse backs up to keep the rope tight. Then he stands still while the rider ties the

Getting off your horse before he comes to a stop saves time in a calf-roping class. (AQHA photo by Wyatt McSpadden)

calf's legs together, and he stays standing there while the rider gets back into the saddle.

Scores for calf roping are between 60 and 80 points. Anything over 70 is a good score.

DALLY TEAM ROPING

One roper on horseback may be able to rope and tie a calf single-handedly. However, when a calf grows up to be a bigger and stronger animal called a steer, it takes more than one horse and rider to catch and hold him. To do that, the horse-show class called dally team roping has teams made up of two riders.

The word dally comes from the Spanish words *de la vuelta*, which mean to take a turn. That's because as soon as a cowboy throws his rope over the steer, he makes one turn of the rope around the saddle horn.

Just like in calf roping, only the horse is judged. In fact, only one horse of the team is judged. It may be the one whose rider is called the header. The header ropes the steer's head. Or it may be the one whose rider is the heeler. The heeler ropes the steer's hind legs down around its heels.

Horses are scored on how they stand in the starting box, how quickly they follow the steer, and how well they stay in position while the rider ropes the steer.

Like in calf roping, horses are scored between 60 and 80 points, with more than 70 points being a good score.

CUTTING

Cattle are herd animals that spend their lives in groups even more than horses now do. They become upset when they're away from other cows, and they'll do just about anything to get back to the herd.

The job of the cutting horse is to move a cow away from the herd and then keep it from going back to the group. What's more, once the rider chooses which cow is to be kept apart, the rider's job is finished. Really! The horse does the rest with no help from the person on his back!

The rider of a cutting horse is called the cutter. The cutter starts by walking the horse into the herd and choosing the cow that the horse should work. Then the cutter puts a big loop in the reins, puts one or both hands on the saddle horn, and lets the horse take over.

When you watch a cutting horse, you'll see how smart a horse can be. He'll drop his head until he's almost eye-to-eye with the cow. Then he waits for the cow to move around him to get back to the herd.

But he doesn't let the cow go by. He blocks the way, and when the cow tries to pass on the horse's other side, the horse blocks that way too. It's just like the way a basketball or a soccer player tries to keep someone on the other team who has the ball from getting to the basket or the goal.

The whole time the cutter keeps on doing nothing, just sitting and watching from what's been called "the best seat in the house."

Each horse has two and a half minutes in the arena. If the cutter thinks the horse has tired out the cow, he or she can move on to another cow if there's enough time left.

Judges give points for how well the horse works the cow. Each horse starts with 70 points, and gets or loses more points depending on how he did.

A good cutting horse has cow sense. That means he can guess what a cow will do, maybe even before the cow knows. Cow sense really can't be taught. A horse either has it or he doesn't.

A cutting horse stays low to the ground so he can quickly move whichever way the cow moves. (AQHA photo by Wyatt McSpadden)

American Quarter Horses have cow sense, and that's what makes them the world's best cutting horses.

TEAM PENNING

As the name tells us, team penning is a team sport. And it's loads of fun.

Each team is made up of three riders. Their job is to separate three cows from a herd at one end of the arena, then move them into a pen at the other end of the arena. The pen is a square area with fences and a gate. Sound easy? It's not, especially when one, two, or even all three cows decide to run back to their friends in the herd.

There are between twenty-one and forty-two cows in the herd. They all have numbers painted on their back. The numbers are in groups of threes: Three cows wear #1, another three wear #2, and so on. Before the event, all the teams draw numbers that match the numbers on the cows.

When a team's turn is called, the three riders come into the arena. The horse-show announcer tells the crowd which number they have picked. Then the fun starts.

Each member of the team has a different job to do. One rider separates the team's three cows from the herd one at a time. Then he or she moves each cow up the arena. Another person on the team moves the cow into the pen. The third person on the team keeps the cows from running back to the herd. That's an important job too, because cows like to be in herds even more than horses do.

This class is called team penning because it takes lots of teamwork. Sometimes a rider needs help. If that happens, he or she yells out. Then the others move around and switch jobs. And since everyone needs to know where the rest of the team is, riders shout out orders too.

Each team has two minutes to move all three cows into the pen—if they can. The team that does it the fastest is the winner.

BARREL RACING

Barrel racing used to be a sport for young girls. Now it's popular with boys and girls, and with men and women too.

Three big barrels are put in the arena in a three-sided pattern. Two barrels are across from each other and the third is the farthest from the line where the riders start and finish.

One at a time, riders race their horses around the barrels in what's called a cloverleaf pattern. Most start by circling around

Horses and riders make tight turns around the barrels in barrel racing. (AQHA photo by Wyatt McSpadden)

the barrel on the right, then moving across the arena to the barrel on the left. They run up and circle around the barrel at the far end, then gallop as fast as they can back across the finish line.

If they wish, they can do the pattern by starting with the barrel on the left.

Although going around the course as fast as you can is important, you want a horse that can make tight turns without knocking over any barrel. That's because knocking over a barrel adds five seconds to the real time the horse takes to go around the course. And since the fastest time wins, having even one barrel down makes a big difference in the final score.

POLE BENDING

Pole bending looks like in-line barrel racing. Six poles are set twenty-one feet apart from each other. One at a time, horses and riders gallop up to the far pole and come back weaving between the poles. When they circle the pole that's closest to the starting and finish line, they zigzag up the line again, turn around the last pole, and gallop down to the finish line.

Horses that are good at pole bending can make very tight turns as they go between the poles. That's important because, like in barrel racing, five seconds are added for any pole that's knocked down. And also like in barrel racing, the horse and rider that finish the course fastest are the winners.

ENGLISH CLASSES

So far we've seen classes that come from the kind of work cowboys did—and still do. Now let's look at the English classes, starting with the hunter division.

The English style of riding that's done at AQHA shows is called hunt seat. This name comes from the sport of fox hunting. In fox hunting, riders follow a pack of foxhound dogs that chase foxes. The hounds and the horses and riders that follow them often run for many miles at a time. The horses have to jump over wooden fences, stone walls, rows of bushes, and anything else that is in their way.

The horses that are used in fox hunting are called hunters. Even though the horses that take part in hunter classes don't really hunt foxes, they jump fences and walls that look like what you find while fox hunting. Some of the fences, or jumps as they are also called, are boxes with bushes on top. Some are wooden blocks that are painted to look like stone walls.

Most fences have poles across their tops. Poles are also called rails. The rails sit in metal cups and come down easily whenever a horse's foot hits them.

A course of jumps is made up of at least eight fences. They are between two feet, nine inches and three feet, nine inches high, depending on the experience of the horses or sometimes the riders in the class. Sometimes, however, hunter classes for very beginning riders have smaller fences.

WORKING HUNTER

In working-hunter classes, horses are judged on how well they go like the kind of horse used in fox hunting. A hunter should jump easily and safely. Because legs that dangle can hit a fence, a hunter should fold his front legs and tuck his hind legs under his body while he jumps.

Leaving the ground too far away from a fence is dangerous because a horse may land on the fence. Leaving the ground too close to the fence may make the horse hit the rails on the way up. That's why hunters lose points for leaving too far back or too close. They also lose points for chipping in, which means adding an extra little step in front of a fence.

A hunter loses even more points by not trying to jump. That can be done either by stopping in front of the fence or by running around it. You wouldn't want to ride a horse like that while fox hunting, would you?

And neither would the person who's judging a working-hunter class.

HUNTER UNDER SADDLE

Because people who go fox hunting spend many hours on their horses, they want ones that are comfortable to ride. In a hunter under saddle class, judges want to see horses with long, low, and comfortable steps at the walk, the trot, and the canter (remember, trot and canter are what Western riders call the jog and the lope).

A hunter's trot should be low, with his front legs swinging straight as if his toes are just brushing the ground. The canter should look just as easy. Some judges ask for a hand gallop. That's a little faster canter, but not too fast.

A hunter should have good manners. Horses lose points for bucking or for trying to kick other horses. You wouldn't want that to happen if you're riding in a group, would you?

HUNTER HACK

Hack is another way of saying "under saddle." In a hunter hack class, horses are judged on how well they jump two little fences and on how well they move at the walk, trot, and canter.

JUMPERS

The horses we see in jumper classes are not judged on how easily or safely they jump. All that counts is not knocking the fences down. That's not so easy, because the fences are bigger than the ones in a hunter class. Jumper fences are from three and a half to four feet high.

Jumpers get points for doing things wrong. These points are called faults. Knocking down a fence is four faults. Not trying to jump a fence is three faults the first time, and another six faults in case the horse refuses a second time. Horses also get faults if they take too long to finish the course.

The people who make up jumper courses put the fences around the arena in places that test how well the horses can jump. Horses do not see the course until they enter the arena for their go-round. However, riders can walk the course before the class. Walking from fence to fence also helps them remember what order they're to jump the fences in.

English riding form and control are judged in a hunt seat-equitation class. (AQHA photo by Wyatt McSpadden)

A go-round where a horse gets no faults is called a clear or a clean round. If two or more horses finish with no faults, there will be another go-round called the jump-off.

Jump-offs are very exciting. Time really counts here. There's a new course, and horses and riders really go fast. That's because if there's another tie score, the winner is the horse that went the fastest.

HUNT-SEAT EQUITATION ON THE FLAT

Equitation is another word for horsemanship. Like in Western horsemanship, riders in hunt-seat equitation classes are judged on how well they sit on a horse and how well they control him.

One at a time, riders do a pattern that the judge has told them to ride. They may have to ride a circle or a figure eight at the trot or the canter, or do even harder things.

Mistakes riders make, like letting their legs flop around instead of staying against the horse's sides, are marked down. So are elbows that don't stay against the rider's sides. Posting on the wrong diagonal at the trot or on the wrong lead at the canter is a very bad mistake.

If the judge can't decide on the winner after watching everyone in the class, he or she can ask for further work.

If you know how to ride English style, you can make believe you're a judge. When you watch a hunt-seat equitation class, ask yourself which rider should get the blue ribbon.

EQUITATION OVER FENCES

As we've learned, "over fences" means jumping. One at a time, the riders take their horses around a course of jumps. There are at least six fences and they're either two feet nine inches or three feet tall.

Judges watch how the riders sit on their horses, especially while they're in the air during a jump. They want to see a rider stay in balance with the horse. Being left behind means being thrown back in the saddle when the horse starts the jump. That's not being in balance.

Just like in hunter classes, a rider who lets a horse chip, or add an extra little step, in front of a fence won't win a top prize. Neither will trotting when the horse should be cantering. Other bad mistakes are losing a stirrup and letting a horse stop in front of a jump.

Like Western horsemanship classes, English-style equitation classes are a great place for you to look for things that will help your own riding. If you see someone who rides well, remember what he or she looks like. Then the next time you're on a horse, try to ride like that person.

PLEASURE DRIVING

If you were living many years ago, you would hitch your family's horse to a wagon. Then you would drive to school or to church, or to go shopping or to visit a friend. That's how everyone got around in the days before there were cars.

Horses in pleasure-driving classes pull two-wheeled carts at the walk, park gait, and road gait. (AQHA photo by Wyatt McSpadden)

Today, instead of wagons, pleasure-driving horses pull two-wheeled carts. The horses move at three gaits: a smooth and lively walk, a trot called the park gait, and a faster trot called the road gait.

After going at all three gaits both ways of the arena, the horses line up until the judge chooses the winner.

Speed isn't important in pleasure driving. In fact, moving too fast is marked down. What judges would rather see are horses that look as though they're doing their job happily and safely.

FOR FURTHER INFORMATION:

Winning with the American Quarter Horse, written by Don Burt, former AQHA President and a leading judge (published by Doubleday in 1996), discusses all the AQHA horse-show divisions and classes from the way a judge sees them. It's a good book for anyone who wants to show or just watch horse shows.

AQHA will send you a booklet called *Your First American Quarter Horse Show* free of charge. It is full of information about getting ready for and riding in horse shows.

Another booklet, *Competitive Horse Judging,* is a guide to becoming a successful horse-show judge.

AQHA offers the following videos:

Best Seat in the House (Cutting): Two trainers of cutting horses explain how to train them. Suitable for beginners and experienced horse enthusiasts. 28 minutes.

The Reining Horse: Two trainers discuss reining as the basis for all performance competition. Also available in Spanish. 25 minutes.

Team Roping: Tips on techniques and timing in team roping competition. Also available in Spanish. 23 minutes.

Working Cow Horse: Three trainers explain and show basic training techniques for a working cow horse. Several reining and cow work performances are discussed. Also available in Spanish. 25 minutes.

Western Horsemanship: This tape gives valuable tips on proper Western horsemanship. Included is a series of exercises designed to build confidence in both horse and rider. There are examples of actual classes to follow. This is an excellent film for youth and amateur competitors. 28 minutes.

Showmanship—The Basics: Grooming and preparation of the horse and exhibitor for showmanship competition. Additionally, many dos and don'ts regarding class rules and routines are covered. 28 minutes.

Team Penning: A leading trainer explains the basics of team penning all the way up to techniques for teamwork and winning runs. He also discusses the qualities of a good team penning horse. 40 minutes.

Hunt Seat Equitation: This video discusses the rider's correct body, hand, and leg position, as well as what to wear and how to do specified movements. 28 minutes.

In the English Tradition, Part I: English riding, especially the hunter under saddle class. Tack and clothing, plus what is expected of hunter under saddle horses. Good for both beginners and experienced riders. Can be shown with or without Part II. 23 minutes.

In the English Tradition, Part II: Basic techniques for a horse learning to jump low fences. Tips on showing and judging horses in hunter hack, working-hunter, and jumper classes. Can be shown with or without Part I. 17 minutes.

Pleasure Driving: Which tack to use and how classes are held, together with examples of pleasure-driving classes. 10 minutes.

Horse Judging, Part I: Halter and reining competition with each class composed of four horses. Viewers have the chance to judge each class before being told the official placings. Explanations for the placings are then given. 46 minutes.

Horse Judging, Part II: In the same format as *Horse Judging, Part I,* this video includes Western pleasure and hunter under saddle competition. 55 minutes.

Horse Judging, Part III: Includes trail and Western riding classes. 45 minutes.

Horse Judging, Part IV: Includes halter and reining classes. 46 minutes.

Judging Roping: This tape includes dally team roping, heading and heeling, and calf roping. There are two actual classes with four horses for the viewer to judge, followed by an explanation of official placings. 33 minutes.

Judging Reining: Like the other judging tapes, this video includes two classes to judge followed by official placings and explanations. 44 minutes.

Judging Working Hunter: Viewers judge two classes and receive an explanation of the official placings. 30 minutes.

Selecting and Showing Western Pleasure Horses: The basics of the Western pleasure horse, including the walk, jog, and lope, as well as manners and way of moving. An introduction to AQHA's most popular event. 55 minutes.

Reining Basics: A roping trainer demonstrates four types of communication cues to the horse by his rider: bridle and rein cues, leg cues, body cues, and voice or sound cues. 55 minutes.

Dally Team Roping: The more advanced team roper will appreciate these tips on improving skills as a team roper. 28 minutes.

Training the Championship Trail Horse: Basic and more advanced methods for trail competition. The viewer learns about various types of obstacles and how to keep a horse from anticipating them. 43 minutes.

Western Riding, A Competitive Edge: Basic methods for success in Western riding classes. The riding pattern, scoring, and correct lead changes are shown. 25 minutes.

Equitation Over Fences: Instruction for equitation over fences class. The video has classes that the viewer can judge. 70 minutes.

Selecting and Showing Hunter Under Saddle Horses: What to look for in a hunter under saddle horse and how the event is judged. 48 minutes.

If you'd like to learn more about any type of AQHA horse-show division, these groups will send you information about their activities:

American Driving Society
PO Box 160
Metamora, MI 48455-0160
phone: (810) 664-8666; fax: (810) 664-2405

American Horse Shows Association
220 E. 42 St.
New York, NY 10017-5876
phone: (212) 972-2472; fax: (212) 983-7286

Intercollegiate Horse Show Association
PO Box 741
Stony Brook, NY 11790-0741
phone: (516) 751-2803; fax: (516) 751-1157

National Barrel Horse Association
PO Box 1988
Augusta, GA 30901-1988
phone: (706) 722-RACE; fax: (706) 722-9575

National Cutting Horse Association
4704 Hwy. 377 S.
Fort Worth, TX 76116-8805
phone: (817) 244-6188; fax: (817) 244-2015

National Reining Horse Association
3000 NW 10th St.
Oklahoma City, OK 73107
phone: (405) 946-7400; fax: (405) 946-8410

National Snaffle Bit Association
1 Indiana Sq., #2540
Indianapolis, IN 46204-2014
phone: (317) 632-6722; fax: (317) 637-9755

U.S. Team Penning Association
PO Box 161848
Fort Worth, TX 76161-1848
phone: (800) 848-3882; fax: (817) 232-4771

13

LET'S GO RACING

Here I am again, Dash for Two Bits. Just kidding—it's really me, Two Bits. But Dash for Two Bits sounds like a racehorse name . . . and I want to take you to a horse race.

Remember when we were learning about the history of the American Quarter Horse? We saw how people in the early days of America liked to race their horses. Well, people still do.

Racing today is very different. American Quarter Horse racing is now held at more than ninety racetracks across North America. And there's more than $50 million in prize money for horses to win.

Even the horses have changed: Today's American Quarter Horses are faster than ever. They can run faster than fifty miles per hour, faster than any other breed of horse! That's why they're called "America's Fastest Athletes."

Good racehorses like to run. You can tell they do from the very first day they follow their mothers out to a pasture. Some baby

horses would rather stand around. Others start running around the field. Which ones do you think would be better at racing?

Like any other horse that will be ridden, the young racehorse learns to wear a saddle and bridle. The less weight a racehorse has on his back, the faster he can go. That's why a racing saddle is very light. It weighs no more than one or two pounds.

The people who ride racehorses are called jockeys. A jockey must be small and light. Jockeys seldom weigh more than one hundred pounds.

After the horse learns to be ridden, he spends lots of time working out on a training track. Sometimes the horse will be galloped by himself. Often he'll run in a group with other young horses.

Even though these workouts are not supposed to be a race, sometimes one horse tries to run faster than his rider wants him to go. And when another horse tries to keep up, the workout becomes a contest. People watching it will say, "Both horses look like they like to run."

Every young racehorse learns about a starting gate. A starting gate makes sure all the horses in a race will start at the same time. Young horses have to get used to the gate's narrow stalls and the loud bell that rings when the doors swing open.

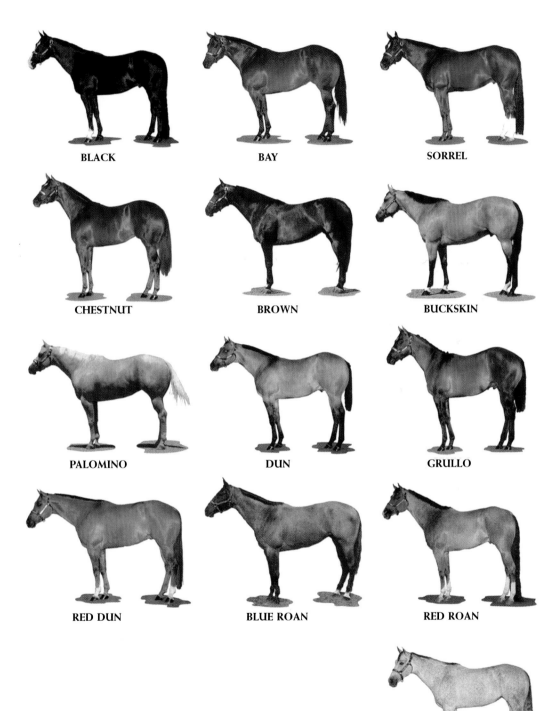

BLACK

BAY

SORREL

CHESTNUT

BROWN

BUCKSKIN

PALOMINO

DUN

GRULLO

RED DUN

BLUE ROAN

RED ROAN

GRAY

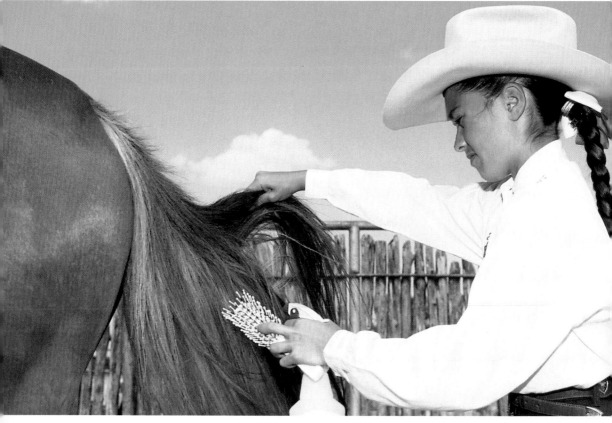

American Quarter Horse racers reach their top speed in just a few strides after leaving the starting gate. (AQHA photo by Wyatt McSpadden)

American Quarter Horses take part in six types of races.

Maiden races are for horses that have never won a race. All American Quarter Horses are called maidens until they win their first race.

Claiming races are a way to buy and sell racehorses. Horses that run in them can be bought, or "claimed," for a certain amount of money, from $1,500 to $50,000 or more!

In allowance and handicap races, the racetrack tells each horse how much weight he must carry. Horses that have won a certain number of races or a certain amount of money will carry more weight. That's because they have shown they're faster than other horses in the race. The more weight a horse carries, the harder it will be for him to win. The extra weight comes from metal bars that go under the horse's saddle.

Stakes races are for the fastest racehorses. They offer large amounts of prize money.

The shortest AQHA races are 220 yards. That's one-eighth of a mile. The longest are 870 yards, or about a half mile.

Most owners like horses that are best at 350, 400, or 440 yards. Races at these distances have the most prize money. On the other hand, many horses like to run shorter distances, and others like longer distances.

A famous race is the All American Futurity at Ruidoso Downs, New Mexico, in September. Another event is the MBNA America® Quarter Horse Racing Challenge Championships. They are run each November and known as "America's Fastest Day of Racing."

You may be wondering what happens to racehorses when they finish racing. Some that have done well become fathers and mothers in order to have children that may also be good racers.

Some racers become reining and roping horses or, because they're fast, barrel-racing and pole-bending horses. Still others become riding or even school horses. Many people have learned to ride on horses that once raced. Maybe you have too.

Cutter and Chariot Racing

A chariot is a kind of two-wheeled wagon. Chariot racing is popular in western states. Two horses work together at pulling the chariot.

The chariots have wire wheels and bicycle tires. They weigh between fifty and sixty pounds.

The people who ride in the chariot and hold the reins are called drivers.

At one end of the course is a starting gate. A quarter mile away is the finish line. Each team of horses and their chariot are put into the starting gate. People called headers make sure the horses are facing straight ahead.

When the starting gate doors spring open, the teams of horses race away. They pull the chariots behind them at speeds of up to forty miles per hour!

The drivers urge their horses to run. The chariots must stay in a straight line from start to finish. Changing lanes is dangerous, and drivers who change lanes will not be allowed to win.

At one time, this kind of racing used sleds called cutters. People who take part in chariot racing are still called cutters.

This list shows the American Quarter Horse racetracks in North America. Which is the closest one to where you live?

Alameda County Fair
Pleasanton, California

Anthony Downs
Anthony, Kansas

Apache County Fair
St. Johns, Arizona

Arapahoe Park
Denver, Colorado

Assiniboia Downs
Winnipeg, Manitoba, Canada

Beulah Park
Grove City, Ohio

Blue Ribbon Downs
Sallisaw, Oklahoma

Brown County Fair
Aberdeen, South Dakota

California State Fair
Sacramento, California

Canterbury Park
Shakopee, Minnesota

Cassia County Fair
Burley, Idaho

Central Wyoming Fair
Casper, Wyoming

Charlie Russell Downs
Great Falls, Montana

Chippewa Downs
Belcourt, North Dakota

Coconino County Fair
Flagstaff, Arizona

Cow Capital Turf Club
Miles City, Montana

Crooked River Roundup
Prineville, Oregon

Dayton Days
Dayton, Washington

Delta Downs
Vinton, Louisiana

Desert Park Exhibition
Osoyoos, British Columbia, Canada

Dixie Downs
St. George, Utah

The Downs at Albuquerque
New Mexico State Fair
Albuquerque, New Mexico

Eastern Idaho Fair
Blackfoot, Idaho

Eastern Oregon Livestock Show
Union, Oregon

Elko County Fairgrounds
Elko, Nevada

Emmett Racetrack
Emmett, Idaho

Eureka Downs
Eureka, Kansas

Evangeline Downs
Lafayette, Louisiana

Evergreen Park
Grande Prairie, Alberta, Canada

Fair Grounds
New Orleans, Louisiana

Fair Meadows
Tulsa, Oklahoma

Fairplex Park
Pomona, California

Fresno District Fair
Fresno, California

Gila County Fair
Globe, Arizona

Gillespie County Fair
Fredericksburg, Texas

Graham County Fair
Safford, Arizona

Grants Pass Downs
Grants Pass, Oregon

Grays Harbor Park
Elma, Washington

Greenlee County Fair
Duncan, Arizona

Hoosier Park
Anderson, Indiana

Hualapai Downs
Kingman, Arizona

Humboldt County Fair
Ferndale, California

Jerome County Fair
Jerome, Idaho

Kamloops Exhibition
Kamloops, British Columbia, Canada

Kin Park
Vernon, British Columbia, Canada

Laurel Brown Racetrack
South Jordan, Utah

Les Bois Park
Boise, Idaho

Lone Oak Racing
Salem, Oregon

Lone Star Park at Grand Prairie
Grand Prairie, Texas

Los Alamitos Race Course
Los Alamitos, California

Louisiana Downs
Bossier City, Louisiana

Manor Downs
Manor, Texas

Marias Fair
Shelby, Montana

Marquis Downs
Saskatoon, Saskatchewan, Canada

Millarville Race Society
Millarville, Alberta, Canada

Mt. Pleasant Meadows
Mt. Pleasant, Michigan

Northwest Montana Fair
Kalispell, Montana

Oneida County Fair
Malad, Idaho

Picov Downs
Ajax, Ontario, Canada

Pocatello Downs
Pocatello, Idaho

Portland Meadows
Portland, Oregon

Prairie Meadows
Altoona, Iowa

Prescott Downs
Prescott, Arizona

Queensbury Downs
Regina, Saskatchewan, Canada

Remington Park
Oklahoma City, Oklahoma

Retama Park
San Antonio, Texas

Rillito Park
Tucson, Arizona

Rossburn Parkland Downs
Rossburn, Manitoba, Canada

Ruidoso Downs
Ruidoso, New Mexico

Rupert Downs
Rupert, Idaho

Sam Houston Race Park
Houston, Texas

San Joaquin County Fair
Stockton, California

Sandy Downs
Idaho Falls, Idaho

San Mateo County Fair
San Mateo, California

Santa Cruz County Fair
Sonoita, Arizona

Solano County Fair
Vallejo, California

Sonoma County Fair
Santa Rosa, California

Sun Downs
Kennewick, Washington

Sunflower Downs
Princeton, British Columbia, Canada

Sunland Park
Sunland Park, New Mexico

Sunray Park
Farmington, New Mexico

Tillamook County Fair
Tillamook, Oregon

Turf Paradise
Phoenix, Arizona

Verendrye Benevolent Association
Ft. Pierre, South Dakota

Waitsburg Racetrack
Waitsburg, Washington

Walla Walla Racetrack
Walla Walla, Washington

Western Montana Fair
Missoula, Montana

White Pine Raceway
Ely, Nevada

Whoop-Up Downs
Lethbridge, Alberta, Canada

The Woodlands
Kansas City, Kansas

Wyoming Downs
Evanston, Wyoming

Yellowstone Downs
Billings, Montana

FOR FURTHER INFORMATION:

For information about American Quarter Horse racetracks or to get the dates of major races, call AQHA at 1-800-414-RIDE.

You will enjoy reading AQHA's *The Quarter Racing Journal* magazine (for subscription information, phone 1-800-291-7323).

AQHA offers a free booklet, *A Guide to Owning Everyone's All American—The Racing American Quarter Horse.*

AQHA also offers the following videos:

The Story of American Quarter Horse Racing: From the colonies of early America to the bright lights of Los Alamitos racetrack, the story of the racing American Quarter Horse is full of excitement. Owners, trainers, and jockeys describe their love of this thrilling sport.

Owning America's Fastest Athlete: What is involved in owning a racing American Quarter Horse. This tape includes the music video "Running Blood."

The Winner's Guide to Wagering: How to handicap (which means to figure out which horse will win). There are separate parts on Thoroughbred and American Quarter Horse racing, making the tape excellent for beginners and experts.

Racing Officials—Their Duties and Responsibilities: The jobs of racing officials during the course of a race day. This tape is excellent for all racing fans.

14

MEET YOUR AQHA

A breed is like a family, but it's also a kind of club. Before any group of horses can be called a breed, people must first agree on what's necessary to be part of the breed.

In the case of the type of horse we've been talking about, several men during the early years of the twentieth century thought that the Steeldust types should be their own breed. A man named "Uncle Billy" Anson wrote about their wide chests and backs and how strong their muscles were. He also wrote about how fast they could run short distances. These looks and skills, Anson said, should make them a special breed of their own.

Another man, Robert M. Denhardt, put together a meeting in Fort Worth, Texas, in 1941. He wanted to put together a special breed list called a registry. Only horses that looked like the Steeldust type could be on that list. These were the horses that later became known as American Quarter Horses.

The group that looked after the list, or registry, was the American Quarter Horse Association. An association is a kind of club. Horses could be on the list only if they could do one of two things. One was to run a quarter of a mile in twenty-three seconds or faster. The other was to show that the horse could work as a ranch horse.

One year later, a horse named Wimpy, owned by the King Ranch of Texas, was chosen as Grand Champion at a special horse show called a stock show, in Fort Worth. That win helped Wimpy become the first horse to be listed in the American Quarter Horse Association registry. When we talk about the American Quarter Horse Association, we often use just the letters AQHA. As you can see, each letter stands for a word in the name of the association.

Other events in AQHA's history show how popular the American Quarter Horse has become:

In 1945, the American Quarter Racing Association was started for people who wanted to use their horses for racing and not for ranch work. It also kept a registry, which gave the names of race-horses and their parents and grandparents too.

In 1946, AQHA moved from Fort Worth to Amarillo, Texas. Two years later, it came out with a magazine called *The Quarter Horse Journal*. More than 70,000 people now receive the magazine by subscription.

During the 1950s, American Quarter Horses became popular in other parts of the country besides the West. In 1955, Go Man Go was named World Champion Quarter Running Horse. He was also World Champion in 1956 and 1957. Because Go Man Go did so well, many people heard about him and became interested in the sport of Quarter Horse racing.

In 1960, AQHA started several programs for children, as well as horse-show classes, or events, for children. This was called a junior horse show.

In 1968, the first All-American Quarter Horse Congress was held in Columbus, Ohio. That was a special meeting and horse show only for people who owned American Quarter Horses. By that time, you could find American Quarter Horses in thirty-eight countries around the world.

In 1970, AQHA created the American Junior Quarter Horse Association to handle programs for people eighteen years old and younger.

In 1974, one million horses were listed in the AQHA registry. That made AQHA the first breed association to have listed that many horses. In addition, 75,000 people had joined AQHA.

In 1977, the Youth Scholarship Program was established. This gave money to children to continue their studies. In 1980, the Youth AQHA Performance Champion Program was started to honor children who did well in horse shows in events for young people.

In 1983, AQHA registered a filly named Two Million, owned by the King Ranch. She had been named that because she was number two million in AQHA's registry.

In 1986, the television show called *America's Horse* first appeared on TV.

In 1991, AQHA opened the American Quarter Horse Heritage Center and Museum, including the American Quarter Horse Hall of Fame, in Amarillo.

Also in 1991, AQHA started a new Horseback Riding Program that gives prizes to people who ride or drive their American Quarter Horses.

That same year, AQHA listed number three million in its registry. That horse was a filly named Three Million Cash.

In 1992, the American Junior Quarter Horse Association World Championship Show moved to Fort Worth, Texas, after eighteen years in Tulsa, Oklahoma.

In 1995, the American Junior Quarter Horse Association started the STAR Program to test how much young horse lovers know about horses.

In 1996, the American Junior Quarter Horse Association got a new name: the American Quarter Horse Youth Association. It is also known as AQHYA.

In 1997, Ride '97, a new national trail ride program, was started for horses of all breeds. This program was introduced in other countries the next year.

In 1998, the sport of reining became the United States Equestrian Team's sixth sport. Equestrian is another word for horseback rider. The United States Equestrian Team puts together groups of horses and riders for important events like the Olympics.

Also in 1998, AQHA started a new magazine called *America's Horse* for all people who are members of the association.

The American Quarter Horse Association is the largest horse breed registry in the world. As of 1999, almost four million American Quarter Horses have been listed in the registry.

About 325,000 people around the world belong to AQHA, and more than one million people own and enjoy American Quarter Horses.

If you and your family are not yet members, please get in touch with AQHA by writing, phoning, or visiting our Web site at www.aqha.org.

FOR FURTHER INFORMATION:

The Quarter Horse Journal and *The Quarter Racing Journal* are printed every month. *America's Horse* is printed every other month. They have stories about what's going on in the American Quarter Horse world and other features—like my Two Bits pages in *The Quarter Horse Journal.* Membership in AQHA includes a subscription to *America's Horse.*

The AQHA offers the following videos:

From the Beginning: Learn how AQHA started. The video has movies that include Wimpy and other old AQHA horses. 24 minutes.

AQHA at a Glance: Learn how the largest horse association in the world helps its members enjoy their horses. 19 minutes.

The American Quarter Horse—You'll Always Remember the Ride: Learn about AQHA shows, races, and programs. 10 minutes.

Inside the American Quarter Horse Heritage Center and Museum: Take a trip through the museum. Learn about shows that include the Hall of Fame. 5 minutes.

AQHYA: Check This Out!: Learn about AQHA's programs for young people. 9 minutes.

So Long, Partners

I had lots of fun telling you about American Quarter Horses and the ways you can have fun with them. There's much more we could talk about, but that would make a book too heavy for you to lift!

Remember, what you've learned in this book is just the start. You can find out more by reading the books and magazines that AQHA has for its members. You'll want to watch their videos too.

When you join the American Quarter Horse Youth Association, you'll meet many other young people like yourself who love horses and riding.

If you've never gone to an AQHA horse show or an American Quarter Horse race, I bet you'll want to after reading this book. Maybe someday you'll show or race an American Quarter Horse yourself!

Okay, I've got to go now. But I'll see you in the pages of *The Quarter Horse Journal.*

Have fun!

Your friend,
Two Bits

A Glossary
of Horse Words

Look at the word alfalfa, the third word on this list. You'll see that it's also written as al-FAL-fa. The part of the word in capital letters is the part that is stressed when you say the word. You'll find other words in the glossary that are written out that way. That's to help you say them correctly.

Words printed in *italics* within a definition can also be found in this glossary.

aged: A horse that is four years or older (also called senior).

aid: A signal that a rider gives a horse to ask him to do something, such as *walk* or *stop*. *Western riders* use the word *cue* to mean the same thing.

alfalfa (al-FAL-fa): A kind of grass that's made into *hay*.

amateur (AM-a-chur): A person who rides or works with horses without being paid for it. The opposite of an amateur is a *professional*.

American Quarter Horse Youth Association: A part of the *American Quarter Horse Association* for young people under the age of eighteen. It's also called AQHYA, the letters that start each word.

AQHA: These four letters are another way of saying *American Quarter Horse Association*.

American Quarter Horse Association: The group that helps American Quarter Horses and the people who own them. It's also called *AQHA*, the letters that start each word.

arena: Another word for a large riding ring, especially one at a horse show.

back cinch: The rear *girth* on a Western *saddle*.

bald face: A wide white *marking* on a horse's face from above the eyes to the bottom of the nose.

bale: A heavy block of *hay*.

barley: A grain that's used as *feed* for horses.

barrel: The middle part of a horse's body, between the front legs and the *hind* legs.

barrel racing: A horse-show event where, one at a time, riders *gallop* their horses around three barrels. The fastest time from start to finish wins.

bars: The spaces between a horse's front and back teeth where the *bit* goes.

bay: The color of a horse that has a brown body and a black *mane* and tail.

bedding: Wood shavings, sawdust, or *straw* that covers the floor of a stall. Bedding makes standing or lying down more comfortable for the horse.

billet (BILL-it): The strap on a *saddle* that the *girth* or the *cinch* buckles to.

bit: The metal part of a *bridle* that goes in the horse's mouth. One end of the *reins* is attached to the bit, and the rider gives the horse *cues* to stop or turn by pulling on the reins.

blacksmith: A person who puts shoes on horses. Blacksmith is another word for *farrier.*

black: The color of a horse that has a black body and a black *mane* and tail.

blaze: A wide white *marking* that goes all the way down the horse's face. A blaze is narrower than a *bald face.*

blue roan: The color of a horse that has a body of white and black hairs and a black *mane,* tail, and legs.

board: The money paid to keep a horse at someone else's stable.

body brush: A brush with thick hair that's used to clean a horse's body.

bosal (bo-SAL): The part of the *hackamore* that goes around the horse's nose.

bounce pad: A foam rubber pad that goes between the *saddle* and the horse's back.

box stall: A square stall in a barn. A box stall is wider and more comfortable for a horse than a straight stall.

bran: A horse *feed* made of the outside part of *oats* or wheat.

breast-collar: Straps that go around a horse's chest and keep the *saddle* from sliding back.

breed: A group of animals from the same family that look alike. The American Quarter Horse is a breed.

bridle: The *tack* that a horse wears on his head to hold the *bit* in his mouth.

brow-band: The part of the *bridle* that goes across the horse's forehead.

brown: The color of a horse that has a brown or black body. His nose is brown, and his *mane* and tail are black.

buckskin: The color of a horse that has a dark yellow or gold body and a black *mane* and tail.

calf roping: A horse-show *class* where a horse is judged on how well he moves to help the rider rope a calf.

cannon: The lower part of a horse's leg, from the *knee* or the *hock* down to the *fetlock.*

canter: The three-beat *gait* known in *Western riding* as *lope.*

cantle (CAN-til): The back part of a *saddle.*

cavesson (CAV-a-son): The part of an English *bridle* that goes around the horse's nose.

Certificate of Registration (sur-TIFF-a-kit of rej-is-TRAY-shun): A paper from *AQHA* that proves that a horse is really an American Quarter Horse. The paper gives the horse's name, the year he was born, and the name of his owner.

champion: The horse or rider that gets the highest score in a horse-show *division.*

chaps (also said as if spelled "shaps"): A kind of leather pants that cover just the rider's legs. Chaps are often worn in certain Western horse-show *classes.*

chariot: A small wagon with two wheels used in *chariot racing.*

chariot racing: Races where teams of two horses pull a *chariot.* The person who drives the chariot is called a *cutter.*

cheeks: The arms on the rings of some *snaffle* bits. They keep the rings from slipping into the horse's mouth.

cheek-piece: The straps on a *bridle* that hold the *bit* in the horse's mouth.

chestnut (CHEST-nut): The color of a horse that has a light brown body, *mane,* and tail. The chestnut color is very close to the *sorrel* color.

chip: To take an extra little step in front of a jump. A horse that chips in a *hunter* class will lose points for not jumping smoothly.

cinch: The strap on a Western *saddle* that goes under the horse's stomach and keeps the saddle in place.

claiming race: A type of horse race. Horses that run in a claiming race are for sale.

class: Each event of a horse show.

clear round: In *jumper* classes, a *go-round* in which the horse doesn't knock down any fences. Also called a clean round.

clover: A kind of grass that's made into *hay.*

colic: The word for a horse's stomach-ache.

colt: A male horse under the age of four.

combination: Two or three fences in a *hunter* or *jumper* class that are close to each other.

conformation (con-for-MAY-shun): How a horse compares to the way a perfect horse should look. A horse that looks like a perfect horse is said to have good conformation. Horses in *halter* classes in horse shows are judged on their conformation.

cooler: A light blanket that keeps the horse from catching a chill.

corn: The same food that people eat that is also fed to horses.

coronet: The part of the foot right above the *hoof.* Also, a white *marking* around the top of the hoof.

corral (kor-AL): Another word for a riding ring or *arena,* or a fenced place where horses are herded together.

course: All the fences in a *hunter* or *jumper* class. If they are jumped out of order, the rider is off course and will receive no score.

cow: The word that cowboys call any kind of cow, steer, or calf.

cow sense: A horse's being able to figure out the next move that a cow, calf, or steer is going to make.

cow work: The second part of a *working cow horse* class, where the horse and rider try to control the cow. See also *dry work.*

crest: The top part of a horse's neck, on either side of the *mane.*

crop: A riding whip that has a wrist strap.

cross-canter: When the front legs *canter* on one *lead* and the *hind* legs canter on the other lead. It's also called cross firing.

cross tie: To tie a horse with two ropes, one on each side of his *halter.*

croup (croop): The top of the horse's back from behind the *saddle* to the tail.

crown-piece (KROWN-peece): The part of the *bridle* that goes over the horse's head, behind his ears.

cue: A Western word for the signals a rider gives the horse. Also called *aid.*

curb: The type of *bit* that has arms called *shanks.* The shanks act as levers and press the bit against the horse's mouth and head. A curb bit almost always has a *port.* Curb bits are usually worn by Western horses.

curb chain or *curb strap:* A chain or strap that goes behind the horse's chin. It is used with a *curb* bit.

curry comb: A metal or hard rubber brush used to scrape dried dirt off a horse's body.

cutter: The person who rides a *cutting* horse. Also, the person who drives the horses in a *chariot race.*

cutting: A horse-show *class* where a horse is judged on how well he moves one cow away from a *herd,* then keeps the cow from running back to the herd. The word cut means to move a cow away from the herd.

dally: To wrap a rope around the saddle *horn* after a steer or calf has been roped. The word comes from the Spanish phrase *de la vuelta* (deh la voo-WELL-ta), meaning to turn the rope.

dally team roping: A horse-show event where a horse is judged on how well he helps his rider rope the head or the *hind* feet of a steer. See the words *header* and *heeler.*

dam: The mother of a horse.

diagonal (di-AGG-uh-null): When a rider *posts* the *trot* and circles to the right, the rider rises out of the *saddle* when the horse's right front leg hits the ground. The rider is then on the left diagonal. Circling to the left, the rider rises when the left front leg hits the ground. The rider is then on the right diagonal. Those are the correct diagonals to be on when trotting in those directions.

division: A group of horse-show *classes* that all have the same event. For example, the *halter* division, or the *trail* horse division.

dock: The thick top part of the tail.

dressage (dre-SAHJ): A French word that means training.

driver: The person who holds the *reins* in a *pleasure-driving* class.

dry work: The first part of a *working cow horse* class, where the horse and rider do a pattern of circles, rundowns, and other movements. The dry work comes before the horse and rider *work the cow*.

dun: A horse with a yellowish or gold body, a black or brown mane and tail, a dark stripe along his back, and stripes on his legs.

earpiece: The part of a Western *bridle* that goes over the horse's ear. It keeps the bridle from slipping off.

English: A style of riding based on jumping. The word is also used to describe the equipment used in this style of riding, such as an English *saddle*.

enter: To sign up for a horse show or race.

entry: A horse that takes part in a horse show or runs in a race.

equine (EE-kwine): Another word for horse.

equitation (eh-kwe-TAY-shun): Another word for *horsemanship*.

equitation over fences: A horse-show *class* where *amateur* or youth riders are judged on how well their horses jump over a *course* of fences.

farrier (FAH-ree-yer): A person who puts shoes on horses. A farrier is sometimes called a *blacksmith*.

fault: A score in a *jumper* class for knocking down a fence or not jumping a fence or going too slowly. The horse that has the fewest faults is the winner.

feed: Grain and other kinds of food that make a horse strong.

fence work: The second part of a *working cow horse* class, when the horse and rider *work* a cow. See also *dry work.*

fender: The wide pieces of leather on the stirrup *leathers* of a Western *saddle.* Fenders keep the stirrup leathers from rubbing against the rider's legs.

fetlock: The part of the horse's lower leg above the foot, where the *pastern* and the *cannon* meet.

field keeping: Keeping a horse in a field or a *pasture* instead of in a barn. Also called *pasture keeping.*

filly: A female horse under the age of four.

flake: A slice of *hay* from a *bale.*

flank cinch: Some Western *saddles* have two *cinches.* The one in back is called the flank cinch or *back cinch.*

float: To smooth down the sharp edges of a tooth.

flying change of lead: At the *lope* or *canter,* going from one *lead* to the other without *trotting* in between. See also *simple change of lead.*

foal: A *colt* or a *filly* that has not yet been taken away from its mother.

forearm (FOR-arm): The upper part of a horse's front leg, between his body and his *knee*.

forehand: The part of the horse's body that's in front of where the *saddle* goes.

foreleg (FOR-leg): Another word for front leg.

forelock (FOR-lock): The part of the *mane* that grows down between the horse's ears.

fork: The front part of a Western *saddle*.

forward seat: A style of *English* riding used for jumping. The name comes from the rider leaning his or her upper body forward to stay in balance with a jumping horse.

frog: The soft, V-shaped part of the bottom of the horse's foot.

gait (gate): The order that a horse's feet hit the ground (see pages 11–13). The American Quarter Horse moves at four gaits: the *walk,* the *jog* (also called the *trot*), the *lope* (also called the *canter*), and the *gallop.*

gallop: The four-beat *gait* a horse does when he's running fast.

gaskin (GAS-kin): The top part of the hind leg, between the body and the *hock.*

girth: The strap on an English *saddle* that goes under the horse's belly and keeps the saddle in place.

go-round: Each rider's turn in a horse-show *class.*

grade: A horse that doesn't belong to any *breed.*

gray: The color of a horse whose body, *mane,* and tail are a mixture of white and dark hairs.

graze: To eat grass.

grazing bit: A *curb* bit that has *shanks* that curve backward. This allows the horse to put his mouth close to the ground to eat grass.

green: A horse that's not yet trained or a horse that's just starting to be trained.

green working hunter: A horse-show *class* for *hunters* that are in their first year of jumping.

grooming: The word for cleaning a horse.

grullo (GROO-lo): The color of a horse that has a light gray body and a black *mane* and tail. The grullo often has a black stripe down his back.

gullet (GULL-et): The open part of a Western *saddle* below the *horn.*

hackamore (HACK-a-more): A kind of *bridle* that has no *bit.* Pulling on its *reins* puts pressure on the horse's nose and *cues* the horse to stop.

halt: To stand still.

halter: The piece of *tack* that goes on a horse's head, for leading or holding the horse. A halter *class* is also another term for a *conformation* class.

hand: A horse's height is measured in hands. One hand is four inches; a horse that is fifteen hands is sixty inches, or five feet, tall. Horses are measured from their *withers* to the ground.

handicap (HAN-dee-cap): A kind of race in which the faster horses carry more weight than the other horses. This gives the slower horses a better chance to win.

handler: The person who shows a horse to the *judge* in a *halter* class.

hay: Dry grass that is fed to horses.

header: In *dally team roping,* the rider who ropes the head of the steer. In *chariot racing,* the header is the person who makes sure the horses are facing straight ahead at the start of the race.

headstall (HEAD-stall): The part of the Western *bridle* that goes over the horse's head and holds the *bit* in the horse's mouth.

heel: The back part of the foot.

heeler: In *dally team roping,* the rider who ropes the steer's back legs.

herd: A group of horses or cows.

hind (HIGHnd): Another word for back, used to refer to back legs and feet.

hip: The widest part of the horse's hindquarters, above the hind legs.

hock: The part of the *hind* leg where the *gaskin* and the *cannon* come together. The hock works like a person's elbow or knee.

hoof: The hard part of the horse's foot.

hoof pick: A metal tool that's used to clean rocks and dirt out of a horse's foot.

horn: The high piece on the front of a Western *saddle.* It's also called the saddle horn.

horsemanship (HORSE-man-ship): The skill to ride well.

hunt-seat equitation: A horse-show *class* where riders are judged on their *English*-style *horsemanship.*

hunter: A horse-show *division* where horses are judged on how smoothly they jump over fences.

hunter hack: A horse-show *class* in which horses are judged two ways: first on how they jump, then on how smoothly they move at the *walk, trot,* and *canter.*

hunter under saddle: A horse-show *class* in which horses are judged on how smoothly they move at the *walk, trot,* and *canter.*

irons: Another word for the *stirrups* on an English *saddle* or a racing saddle.

jockey (JOCK-ee): The person who rides a horse in a race.

jog: The Western word for *trot,* especially a slow trot.

judge: The person who chooses the winners at a horse show.

jump-off: If two or more horses in a *jumper* class finish the first *go-round* with the best score, they do another go-round called the jump-off. The horse that finishes with the fewest *faults* in the fastest time is the winner.

jumper: A horse-show *division* where horses are scored on how many fences they jump without knocking them down.

keeper: The little leather circle on a *bridle* that holds the end of a strap so that the strap doesn't flap around.

knee: The part of the front leg where the *forearm* and *cannon* come together.

knee roll: The part of some English *saddles* where the rider's knees rest.

lame: Having trouble moving because of a sore leg or foot.

latigo (LAT-a-go): The strap that holds the *cinch* on a Western *saddle*.

lead: The leading front foot at the *lope* or *canter*. A horse lopes or canters on either his right or his left lead. When he circles to the left, he should be on his left lead; going to the right, he should be on his right lead.

lead shank: A strap or rope that snaps to the *halter*. A person holds the other end to lead a horse.

leather: The strap that holds the *stirrup*.

leather dressing: A cleaner that puts oil back in dry or dirty leather.

loin (loyne): The part of the horse's back between the *barrel* and the *hip*.

lope: The three-beat *gait* of a horse. In *English*-style riding, the lope is called the *canter*.

maiden race: A race for horses that have never won a race.

mane: The hair that grows along a horse's neck.

mare: A female horse that's older than three years old.

marking: A white patch or stripe on a horse's face or leg. See *bald face, blaze, coronet, pastern, snip, sock, star,* and *stocking*.

martingale (MAR-tin-gale): The strap that goes from the *girth* to the *bridle* and passes between the horse's front legs. A martingale keeps a horse from lifting his head up in the air.

mouthpiece (MOUTH-piece): The part of the *bit* that goes in the horse's mouth.

muck out: To clean manure out of a stall.

mustang (MUSS-tang): The wild (meaning not owned and not tamed) horse of the American West.

near: The left side of a horse.

neck-rein: To lay a *rein* on the horse's neck as a signal to turn. For example, to turn to the left, you lay your right rein against his neck.

neigh (nay): The sound a horse makes when he's talking. Also called *whinny*.

oats: A kind of grain used as *feed*.

off: The right side of a horse.

overreaching: When a horse's *hind* feet hit the back of his front feet, usually while *trotting*. In some parts of the country, it's called forging (FOR-jing).

oxbow (OKS-bo): A kind of Western *stirrup* that has a round bottom.

oxer (OCK-sir): A wide jump in a *hunter* or *jumper* class.

palomino (pal-a-MEE-no): The color of a horse that has a golden yellow body and a white *mane* and tail.

park gait: In *pleasure-driving* classes, the *trot* that is slower than the *road gait.*

pastern (PASS-turn): The part of the lower leg between the *fetlock* and the foot. Also, a white *marking* around the pastern.

pasture: (PASS-chur): A fenced-in field where horses can live.

pasture keeping: Keeping a horse in a *pasture* or field. Also known as pasturing or *field keeping.*

pattern: The order in which horses do required movements in certain horse-show *classes.*

pleasure driving: A horse-show *class* where horses pull two-wheeled carts. The horses are judged on how well they move at the *walk, road gait,* and *park gait.*

pole bending: A horse-show *class* in which horses and riders race around six poles and try not to knock any over. The fastest time wins.

poll (pole): The part of the head between the ears. The poll is the highest part of a horse.

pommel (POM-el): The front part of the *saddle.*

port: The raised part of the *mouthpiece* of a *curb* bit. The port often looks like an upside-down letter U.

post: To move up and down in the *saddle* when the horse *trots.* Posting makes trotting more comfortable.

professional (pro-FESH-in-el): A person who is paid to work with horses and riders.

program: A book that lists the horses and riders that are taking part in a horse show or horse race.

pulling: Making a *mane* and tail shorter and thinner by removing hairs.

purse: The prize money in a horse-show *class* or horse race.

rail: (1) The outer edge of the inside of an *arena;* (2) one of the poles across the top of fences that *hunters* and *jumpers* try to jump over.

rasp: A file used to *float* teeth.

rate: In *working cow horse* and roping *classes,* to speed up or slow down to keep up with a cow.

red dun: The color of a horse that has a light yellow body, a red stripe down his back, and a red or white *mane* and tail.

redtop (also called redtip): A kind of grass used as *hay.*

red roan: The color of a horse that has a body of white and red hairs.

registry (REJ-is-tree): A special list of horses that belong to the same *breed.* The *AQHA* keeps the registry of American Quarter Horses.

reins: The straps that go from the *bridle* to the rider's hands. Reins are used to turn and stop the horse.

reining: A horse-show *class* where horses are judged on how well they do *patterns* of circles, spins, stops, and other movements.

reserve (ree-ZURVE): The horse or rider that gets the second-highest score in a horse-show *division.*

rigging: The position of a *cinch* on a Western *saddle.*

road gait: In *pleasure-driving* classes, the *trot* that is faster than the *park gait.*

rollback: A movement in *reining* where the horse stops, turns back, and then moves off, all without stopping.

romal (ro-MAL): A kind of Western *rein* that has two straps that come together to become one rein.

rundown: A *reining* movement where the horse runs from one end of the ring to the other.

saddle: The piece of *tack* that the rider sits on.

saddle soap: A special soap for cleaning *tack* and other leather.

saddlery shop (SAD-le-ree): See *tack shop.*

seat: The part of the *saddle* where a rider sits. Also, how well a rider rides a horse, as in the saying, "He has a good seat."

shank: The long metal arms of a *curb* bit that hold the *reins.* Also, a strap or rope for leading a horse that's wearing a *halter* (also called *lead shank*).

shoulder: The part of the horse's body between his neck and where the saddle goes.

showmanship (SHOW-man-ship): A kind of *halter* class where youth and *amateur* exhibitors are judged on how well they show their horses to the judge.

side-check: A strap or rope that runs from the *saddle* to the *bridle.* It keeps the horse from putting his head down to *graze.*

silks: The shirt and cap worn by *jockeys.* Owners of racehorses have silks in different colors and patterns that help people watching a race tell the horses apart.

simple change of lead: When a horse *trots* or *walks* while changing *leads* at the *lope* or *canter,* he's doing a simple change of lead. (If he changes without trotting or walking, he's doing a *flying change of lead.*)

skirt: The part underneath the *cantle* on a Western *saddle* or over the stirrup *bars* on an English saddle.

snaffle (SNAFF-ul): A *bit* that has no *shanks*. A snaffle can have a straight *mouthpiece* or a mouthpiece that bends in the middle.

snip: A white *marking* near the horse's nose.

sock: A white *marking* from the foot to about halfway up the horse's lower leg. See *stocking*.

sole: The bottom of a horse's foot.

sorrel (SOR-ul): The color of a horse that has a red-brown body, *mane*, and tail. More American Quarter Horses are sorrel than any other color.

sound: Another word for healthy.

spin: A *reining* movement where the horse turns completely around one or more times while keeping one *hind* foot on the ground.

split reins: Reins that are not tied together. Most Western-style reins are this type.

stallion: A male horse that's three years or older.

star: A white *marking* above a horse's eyes.

stifle: The part of the horse where the *gaskin* meets the body.

stirrup: A metal or wood loop attached to the *saddle* for the rider's foot.

stocking: A white *marking* from the foot up to the *knee* or the *hock.* A stocking is longer than a *sock.*

stop: In *reining* and *working cow horse* classes, the movement where the horse slides to a halt.

straw: Dry grass that's used as stall *bedding.*

stretch: The straight part of the racetrack that ends at the finish line.

stride: Each of the steps a horse takes at a *gait.*

strip: A narrow white *marking* that runs from above a horse's eyes to his nose.

sweat scraper: A long and thin metal tool that's used to wipe away water after a horse has had his bath.

sweet feed: Grain that's mixed with a sugar product.

tack: Saddles, bridles, halters, and other things that horses wear to be ridden or led.

tack shop: A store that sells things for horses and riders. Also called a tack store or *saddlery shop.*

tapadaros (tap-a-DARE-ohs): Also known as taps. The part of some Western *stirrups* that covers the front of the stirrup.

team penning: A horse-show event for teams of three riders. Each team moves three cows from a *herd* into a pen at the far end of the ring. The team that moves its cows the fastest is the winner.

Thoroughbred: A *breed* of horse that is good at racing long distances.

throat latch: The strap on the *bridle* that goes under a horse's throat.

thrush: A disease of the *frog* of the horse's foot.

tie-down: A Western word for *martingale.*

time fault: Horses in *jumper* classes must finish the *course* within a certain number of seconds. If they take longer, they are given time *faults* as part of their score.

timothy (TIM-o-thee): A kind of grass used as *hay.*

toe: The front part of the horse's *hoof.*

trail: A horse-show *class* where horses are judged on what they'd be like if ridden on a real trail ride.

trainer: The person who gets horses ready for racing or horse shows. Some trainers teach people to ride.

tree: The frame of a *saddle.*

trot: The two-beat *gait* that's also known as the *jog.*

tush: One of the four extra teeth of a male horse.

vaquero (va-CARE-o): The Spanish word for cowboy.

vertical (VERT-a-kel): A narrow fence in a *hunter* or *jumper* class.

veterinarian (veh-tuh-ruh-NAIR-ee-in): A doctor who helps animals. Often called a vet.

Visalia (vis-a-LEE-a): A Western *stirrup* that's shaped like a bell.

walk: The four-beat *gait* that's the slowest of all a horse's gaits.

Western horsemanship: A horse-show *class* where riders are judged on their form and control.

Western pleasure: A horse-show *class* where horses are judged on how comfortable they are to ride.

Western riding: A horse-show *class* where horses are judged on their *gaits* and how well they change *leads*.

whinny (WIN-ee): The sound a horse makes when he's "talking." Also called *neigh*.

withers (WITH-ers): The highest part of a horse's back, in front of where the *saddle* goes.

work: To move a cow around the *arena*, as the word is used in Western horse shows.

working cow horse: A horse-show *class* where horses are judged first on *reining* movements and then on how well they *work* a cow.

working hunter: A horse-show *class* where horses are judged on how smoothly they jump fences.

worming: Giving a horse medicine to get rid of any worms or insects he might have eaten by mistake.

yearling: A horse between the ages of one and two years.